Keep On Going

The History of
The Bell Tower on 34th

By Roger C. Igo

STELLAR
COMMUNICATIONS
HOUSTON

Hardcover ISBN: 978-1-944952-27-3
E-book ISBN: 978-1-944952-28-0
Library of Congress Control Number 2019940989

For my successors:
I hope and pray you understand
and remember where and how it all started.

Christina and Preston,
Nothing is impossible when you
work hard, pray, and never quit.
Keep on going. I love you!

Because "Our goal is to deliver excellent events
no one will ever forget," proceeds from this book
will go to the Alzheimer's Association.
I hope and pray they find a cure.

Alzheimer's Association
www.alz.org
225 North Michigan Avenue
Floor 17
Chicago, IL 60601
Tel: (312) 335-8700
EIN: 13-3039601

CONTENTS

PREFACE

When I started working on this book, my goal was to share the history of our wedding and special events venue, The Bell Tower on 34th.

I wanted readers to know about The Bell Tower's many ties to Texas history, about the strategies and approaches that made this venue a success, and about my personal journey as The Bell Tower's founder and CEO.

But in the final stages of writing and editing, I realized I'd left something out. Something important. There's a theme to our venue's history: Keep on going.

That simple message is so integral to the legacy of The Bell Tower on 34th that we named the venue's holding company Keep On Going, LLC. The name speaks to the many obstacles that my wife, Angela, and I overcame to get to where we are today. It's also a play on our last name, Igo. (I-go, get it?)

In any case, I realized that if I share anything through this book, "Keep on going" should be at the top of the list. It's one of the most valuable pieces of advice that I can offer you. *Don't lose hope. There is a God, and there is such a thing as a miracle. Whatever your obstacles are, no matter how bad your situation seems, keep on going. Don't give up.*

To be clear, I'm not saying that if you just believe, you'll always achieve your goals. But if the stories in this book prove anything, it's that when you dig your heels in, when you cling to your faith and fight for what you want, *it is possible to overcome great obstacles.*

The chapters that follow are filled with real-life examples of that truth, from leaders and pioneers who've earned a place in history to everyday people—including me—who achieved their goals because they refused to give up.

So, yes, I want to share the amazing history of The Bell Tower on 34th with you. But I also hope that the many accounts of grit and stick-to-it-iveness described here will empower you to keep on going when you encounter challenges of your own.

ACKNOWLEDGMENTS

It was more than 10 years ago when we had lost it all, and no one knew what was going to happen or how things were going to turn out. If it wasn't for the prayers of my mother, the support of my wife Angela, and grace and blessings from God, there would be no story of this very special place called The Bell Tower on 34th. Thank you, Mom. Thank you, Angela. Thank you, God.

I would like to thank and acknowledge Angela, Christina, Preston, Dr. Eriko (Mom) and Mr. Randall Valk, Lydia and George Igo, Glenda and Doug Nicholson (Glenda, your eye for design and contributions of color and style will live on), Bunkie and Nick Nicholson, Maggie and John Nicholson, Natalie and Andrew Clark, Heather and Chad Swannie, Ryan Winkelmann, Sheri Moon, Kenze and Dan Beyer, Carolina Chavez, Heather Donnelly, Felix Ramirez, Pedro Ixquiactap, Sarah Turner, Randall Klein, Mike Kaarafarni, Eloy

Perez, and Christopher Leverett (may God rest his soul). *Thank you for your endless unconditional love and support!*

To the Kempner families: Branch, I will never forget the long hours we spent together on this project. You are one of the smartest people I have ever met. Thank you for all you did and your concern for the details to ensure our launch was a success. Shrub, your wisdom runs deep and wide. Thank you for taking the risk and seeing the possibilities. I learned so much from you both. Thank you!

To Scott Odom, Daniel Sanders, Shahrukh Sanjana, Cory Andrews, Brent Reyburn, Julio Chavez, Chris Higueros. *Thank you all for your belief and trust in me.* You helped us transform a tragedy into something beautiful and amazing.

Tiny positive words of encouragement can be life-changing even when you may not realize your kind words are making an impact on a person. Chuy Terrazas, III, Bill Hibbler, Chad Strader, and Larry Janda, you each gave me just the right words of encouragement at exactly the right time and you truly made a difference. *You have no idea.* Johnny Carrabba, thank you for playing along and for your generosity. I'm sure you had no idea. Frankie B. Mandola, now in heaven, thank you for listening and offering your business advice and encouragement. Bruce Molzan and Robert Guillerman, thank you for the ad hoc meetings, which gave me momentum. Lura Lovestar, thank you for the positive energy. Also, to our neighbors Bob Thomas and

Jacob Ponniah (the antique dealer) for the extra words of encouragement. In those moments when it seemed there were no real solutions, God put you in front of me. Thank you all!

Also, a few words about prayer. The Bell Tower on 34th is proof of its power. I would like to acknowledge Mom's prayer network, which she calls *Circle of 12*. It consists of 12 prayer warriors, who each have their own group of 12 members. Then each of the 12 has a group of 12, and so on. According to Mom at this writing, there are 432 groups worldwide. It's not on Facebook or social media.... just people committed to pray around the clock. *Thank you, Circle of 12, for your prayers! Thank you to each person not in the Circle of 12 who offered your prayers. Thank you to those of you who prayed, and continue to pray, when we didn't ask or even know you were praying. Remember the POWER of prayer!*

I would like to acknowledge the events community and the people of Houston for allowing us to be a different and a disruptive kind of venue unlike any other. We had no sure way of knowing how or if our concept of a venue would be acknowledged, accepted, or embraced. Thank you!

There are also so many talented and diligent employees, past and present, who helped the company grow even after we opened. You are hard-working, enthusiastic, loyal, dedicated, and trustworthy self-starters who make The Bell Tower on 34th an amazing company. Thank you!

Many, many other people also gave me hope and emotional support, which kept me going in my most challenging moments before we ever even knew it might be possible to open our doors and operate as a venue. No matter what, you offered your prayers and support unconditionally. I want to thank you for your amazing love, loyalty, and grit through it all. Thank you for seeing the vision, believing in me, and having the faith to help make the impossible into a reality even though it seemed the world was against us.

I would also like to acknowledge and thank Flori Meeks for your years of hard work and diligence in research for historical accuracy and fact-finding while we worked on this project. Writing this story would not have been possible without your help and guidance.

HEARTACHE IN HOUSTON

Stories started surfacing in fall 2008 about Houston brides-to-be, more than 30 of them, who shared a common tale of loss, betrayal, and heartbreak. And people were pointing the finger at me.

I believe the real culprit here was an evil businessman. He'd promised the brides discounts if they reserved his Houston-based wedding venue with cash. Later, he spent their money and left town. Weeks later, both his existing venue, and a new one he was building in north Houston, had closed their doors.

The businessman's actions wreaked havoc in many lives, from employees, to corporate clients, to vendors.

As for the brides-to-be, women who came to be known as The Brides of Harris County, it seemed as if they were left with no place to hold their weddings and no money left to pay for another location. Their horrible, nightmarish stories made the national news and inspired public outrage, sympathy, and ultimately, a fairy godmother in the form of TV cook and talk show host Rachel Ray. Many of the brides accepted her invitation to participate in a beautiful televised group wedding at Houston's baseball stadium, Minute Maid Park, in November 2008. It was fantastic.

Meanwhile, because of the actions of the evil businessman who left town, his company was forced into bankruptcy that year.

And that's when I joined the ranks of The Brides of Harris County.

True, I was a builder, not a bride. I was the naive contractor overseeing the construction of the evil businessman's new venue in Houston's Garden Oaks neighborhood. And while I had nothing to do with how he ran his businesses, the aftermath of his unthinkable and irresponsible actions sparked a devastating chain reaction that plunged me into one of the most difficult periods of my life.

As one of the venue's unpaid creditors, my successful company and excellent business reputation suffered painful blows. My financial future and ability to provide for my family were on thin ice. And for a while, I couldn't begin to imagine a positive end to my horrible situation.

Unlike The Brides of Harris County, I didn't get a last-minute rescue from an amazing TV fairy godmother. But, through the grace of God, the support of my wife, and the prayers of my mother, I did get a happily-ever-after ending. Or maybe a happy new beginning—one involving our own events venue— would be a more fitting description.

What follows is my perspective of how it all came together and how we managed to keep on going. Some people's names have been changed, but the rest of the story, at least from my point of view, is accurate.

Chapter 1

WELCOME TO THE BELL TOWER ON 34TH

B IG THINGS HAPPEN HERE. THEY REALLY do. Life-changing events of all kinds.

Couples exchange wedding vows. Milestones are commemorated. Corporations introduce new products and announce mergers. We inspire everlasting connections here.

All of that, and more, occurs at The Bell Tower on 34th nearly every day. We've hosted thousands of beautiful weddings and amazing events since we opened in 2009.

I need you to know what made the venue we have today possible—and about a legacy that goes back far beyond our first day of business.

The history of this place has ties to key events and figures dating back to the early days of Texas. It's a tale of spectacular leaps of faith, grit in the face of hardship—and even some frightening moments. The people who hold events here, in most cases, major life events, should know what makes The Bell Tower on 34th special.

I also want to share my role in the venue's history: the seemingly overwhelming obstacles I've faced, along with the special prayers, tenacity, and support that made it possible for me and The Bell Tower on 34th to stand on solid ground today. Maybe these stories will help others, when they're starting to run out of hope, to keep on going and imagine a much brighter future.

OUR VENUE

A lovely shot of The Bell Tower on 34th.

Since we opened The Bell Tower on 34th, we've been striving to maintain a delicate balance. We want and need the venue to evoke a sense of beauty and elegance, to be the kind of place where people can envision their fairy-tale wedding. But we also have worked to make the venue a perfect setting for a Fortune 500 company's strategy session.

That's not to say we haven't woven in distinctive design elements here. What we have is a mixture of influences and styles that work to amplify the beauty, the energy, and the excitement found within our walls on any given day.

If you have ever visited The Bell Tower on 34th, you probably have been struck by the powerful visual impact of the eclectic architecture, private courtyards, and fountains at our venue. Together, they contribute to the feel of an Old World estate or Mediterranean villa. The sweeping staircases, archways, and marble floors have a magical, Hollywood quality. And we've worked in other special touches, as well, including towering, hand-carved wooden doors, Travertine floors, reclaimed brick walls, hand-set Cantera stone walls and patios, and wrought-iron chandeliers.

And there are modern elements, too, like our 30-foot water wall and the state-of-the-art lighting and sound systems.

I'll take you on a more detailed tour of The Bell Tower on 34th, the tour that I usually reserve for prospective clients, later in the book. But first, you may be wondering: Does The Bell Tower on 34th have a real bell tower? Of course it does!

SOUNDS OF JOY

A glimpse of the antique bells in our bell tower.

Not only does The Bell Tower on 34th have a bell tower—it has working antique bells. A few years after we opened, we installed microphones in the bell tower so our guests could hear them from inside the building.

Traditionally, churches have rung bells for centuries, as early as the fifth century in Italy and the seventh century in England. The bells were rung to summon people to church and again to let them know services were starting.

Here at The Bell Tower on 34th, some brides ask for bells to beckon guests inside for the wedding ceremony, and possibly to signal the ceremony is starting. But those practices have been rare.

For the most part, couples opt for the bells to ring right after the groom kisses the bride, or after the new husband and wife are introduced to their guests as a married couple for the first time.

The bell ringing, combined with the right lighting, the scent of the flowers, and other sensory input, can be so powerful that it makes the hairs on the back of your neck stand up. It evokes strong emotions and adds to the impact of the moment.

OUR NEIGHBORHOOD

One of the things that makes The Bell Tower on 34th special is our location. Our venue sits in the fourth-largest city in the United States, a thriving, rapidly growing town that's constantly re-inventing itself. But our venue's northwest Houston neighborhood, Garden Oaks, has the peaceful feel of an established, historic community. Garden Oaks, which was developed in 1937, is known for its old-growth oak, pecan, and magnolia trees, along with curvy streets and an eclectic mix of restored bungalows, plantation- and ranch-style houses, and newly constructed homes.

Today, Garden Oaks has 1,400 homes and still retains some of the small-town feel it had in its early years. While Garden Oaks is largely a bedroom community, it has parks, churches—many with interesting histories of their own—shopping centers, and schools.

In recent years, the neighborhood has been attracting increasing numbers of young families, and in 2013, *Houstonia* magazine named Garden Oaks one of the city's 25 hottest communities.

THE HEART OF WHO WE ARE

From the beginning, my main goal for The Bell Tower on 34th has been to provide excellence in every way possible. It's written into our mission: "We deliver excellent events no one will ever forget."

What does that look like? I tell customers to think back to a powerful sermon or speech they've heard, or maybe an amazing movie or roller coaster ride. At the end, they probably think, "Wow! That was awesome!" They feel inspired. They're pumped. That's what we work to create for our guests. At each event. Every day.

I try to instill that objective into the mind of every employee and stakeholder. It begins during our new employee orientation, when I make everyone in the room recite our pledge. Then, because they rarely say it loudly enough, I have them repeat it.

And, really, that "wow" feeling I'm describing is for employees as well as guests. We want our staff, when they leave for the night, to be able to say, *"I was there. That really was awesome."*

I'm convinced that achieving those moments requires more than staff members committed to creating excellent experiences. We need people committed to achieving that objective *together* for it to work. It's a group effort, and every member of the group should be able to count on the others to help them attain their shared goal.

What I'm talking about is trust. And, just like The Bell Tower on 34th mission, trust is a concept woven

Our team in 2013.

into our company culture. So, during new employee orientations, I also instruct our new hires to turn to the person next to them and say, "I've got your back." Then they say the same to the person on the other side.

I tell people, if you don't feel you can trust your co-workers, you've got to leave. And employees take that to heart. In almost every case, when people realize they don't feel that kind of trust, or they aren't as committed to excellent events as much as the others, they choose to give their notice. In some cases, if they're taking too long to come to that conclusion, or act on it, I step in and ask them to leave.

What we have at The Bell Tower on 34th is special: The whole staff wants each event to be successful, and we're all in it together. You'd be hard pressed to go to a hotel and get that. You can't find it at venues that rely solely on staffing agency workers: Most of those people are just there for the paycheck, not to make a difference in their customer's event.

Our people are here because they're getting a chance to be part of something special like a closely knit family. And, together, they get to make something unforgettable happen.

MASTER STAGE CREW

When we first opened The Bell Tower on 34th, I used to refer to event nights as "organized chaos." That's because it took us a while to learn to manage all of the moving parts of holding a special event, let alone multiple events taking place at the same time. These days, I can confidently say that we can do this. We do it well.

From the moment people arrive, valets direct them to the correct locations. We have staff members tearing down and setting up tables and place settings; perfecting sound and lighting; adjusting the air or heat settings; serving drinks, appetizers, and meals; and choreographing the event's progression, among many, many other steps. And as each event progresses from phase to phase, possibly moving from room to room, our staff is communicating. They're using well-rehearsed processes and relying on multiple contingency plans to ensure seamless transitions—transitions that, ideally, guests don't think twice about. I think of it like theatre stage hands, transforming a set between scenes, or a racing pit crew, servicing a car and getting it back on the track within seconds.

Just like I want customer events to be a success, it's important to me to help our employees succeed at their jobs and the art of juggling multiple special events. We actually hold rehearsals, where we instruct employees to set up a room, break it down, and re-set it while they're being timed.

And during our own company holiday parties, for fun we have had waiter races. Our wait staff breaks off into teams and competes to see who is the fastest setting up tables, complete with linens, plates, forks, stemware, poured water…you get the idea. We time the teams, and the winners receive cash and prizes. While these games are competitive, team members support and encourage each other on the job. Again, they're working together to achieve the same goals.

The result has been the ability to host multiple simultaneous events, flawlessly. I don't think any other venue in Texas has that know-how and ability to the extent that we do. What we have here is special.

SUPPORTING OUR GUESTS

Our customers have valet and a wait staff at their disposal during their events, but that's only part of the picture. We've developed a considerable team of staff members to support our customers' goal. Again, their mission is to make sure that customers have successful events. That team includes event producers who can help customers plan weddings, parties, and other special events. They've told me the work is never boring. They're sounding boards when customers need suggestions. And when customers start getting stressed, they provide shoulders to lean on.

I love seeing our staff go the extra mile for our customers. Take our technology crew. They've developed two special features for customers. Our Bell Tower Customer Hub, an online tool, helps clients manage their events. They can use it for making payments, scheduling tastings and bridal portraits, viewing their menus and floor plans, and checking their event timeline.

The other special feature is our online knowledge base, which comprises the many questions we've received over the years and our detailed answers. It's sort of an FAQ section on steroids. And the knowledge base is intuitive. As customers start typing a question, it starts suggesting matching topics.

We've also developed a client card for each of our customers that entitles them to special deals from a list of approved and insured vendors. Returning clients can also use the card for a financial discount on their next event, and card-holders can pass the card down to later generations.

PART OF THE STORY

As you've probably noticed, once someone is hired by The Bell Tower on 34th, we require them to attend one of our new employee orientations as well as attend our bi-annual company meetings. In most cases, the new hires are expecting to hear a long list of company rules and a rundown of their job responsibilities.

So, at the annual meeting, when I start a slide show that usually includes a black and white photo of a small, solemn, girl beside her mother, I tend to get confused looks from the crowd. Personal shots like that picture— the little girl is my mom—are intermingled with images related to The Bell Tower on 34th's history.

This little girl is my mother, then Eriko Amano, with her mom in Japan.

Each photo has a purpose and a story behind it, but together, the images convey a message: *Once you're part of The Bell Tower on 34th family, you should know our business' story and philosophy. And…it's impossible to separate the story of our business from the story of me, Roger Igo. They're forever intertwined.*

So, what should you know about me? I'll go into more detail later in this book, but in a nutshell, I grew up in the Houston area and am an entrepreneur, a husband, and a father. And as you'll see, I'm never satisfied with status quo. I'm all about pushing ahead, solving problems, and building upon successes. On trying new experiences and learning. And building up others: I love helping other people achieve their dreams and encouraging them to press on in the face of adversity. As for my career journey, I've been a musician, band manager, and music industry advisor, along with a realtor and a developer before beginning my chapter with The Bell Tower on 34th.

I consider launching this business and making it successful some of my greatest accomplishments, despite the painful moments that came with them. But I'll get back to those soon.

Bell Tower Trivia

THE BELL TOWER ON 34TH WAS FEATURED IN THE *HOUSTON CHRONICLE* A FEW YEARS AGO AFTER A COUPLE HOSTED A HARRY POTTER-THEMED WEDDING COMPLETE WITH FLYING OWLS, FLOATING CANDLES, AND QUIDDITCH HOOPS. THE COUPLE RE-CREATED THE FORBIDDEN FOREST AND GREAT HALL AT HOGWARTS SCHOOL FOR THEIR BIG DAY.

Chapter 2

TIES TO TEXAS HISTORY

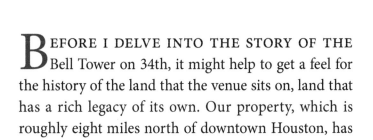

BEFORE I DELVE INTO THE STORY OF THE
Bell Tower on 34th, it might help to get a feel for
the history of the land that the venue sits on, land that
has a rich legacy of its own. Our property, which is
roughly eight miles north of downtown Houston, has
ties to key figures and moments from the histories of
Texas and Houston, dating back to the time when Texas
was a province of Mexico.

I learned about our land's history shortly after we
became owners of The Bell Tower on 34th and paid
Stewart Title Company for a title search, called an
abstract of title, on the property. Within the huge stack
of documents sent to me was an amazing artifact: a
handwritten Mexican land grant dating back nearly
two centuries.

A little background: The Mexican government between 1821 and 1835 used land grants—a transfer of land ownership rights—to entice desirable settlers to the then sparsely populated province of Texas (known at that time as Coahuila-*Tejas)*. Grant holders agreed to become Mexican citizens and take an oath of loyalty to the Mexican government.

The grant I received, dated July 7, 1824, was awarded to American farmer William P. Morton. Strangely, it was for land southwest of The Bell Tower on 34th location, an entire county to the southwest. The grant's writing, in English and Spanish, had faded over the years, but my eyes almost immediately caught one of the signatures: Stephen F. Austin. If you haven't heard of him, he's better known around here as the "Father of Texas."

Whether it was the historical significance of my new treasure trove of documents or the mystery tied to the oldest of them, I was hooked. When I wasn't immersed in the business of running The Bell Tower on 34th, I found myself online, researching land grants and our property's place in Texas history.

THE AUSTIN LEGACY

Texas takes its legacy seriously. If you grow up here, your social studies education doesn't stop with U.S. and world history. You also study Texas history extensively in elementary and middle school. And Stephen Fuller Austin's name comes up frequently. He's best known

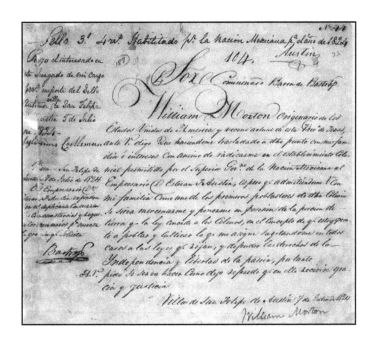

The 1824 land grant I have is written in English and Spanish and includes the signature of Stephen F. Austin, who signed in Spanish as "Estevan."

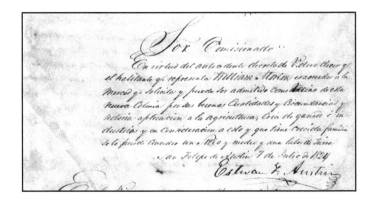

for establishing the first and largest Anglo-American colony in Texas during the 1820s. The modern-day capital of Texas is named for him, along with a state university and a long list of streets, parks, and schools. So, for a native Texan like me, seeing Stephen F. Austin's signature on property documents was a pretty big deal.

I have to say that while Stephen gets the glory for his role in Texas history, at least some of the credit should be shared with his father, Moses Austin. Moses was the one who developed the idea for colonizing Texas, then a territory of Spain, with Anglo-Americans in the first place. Moses was the epitome of grit and stick-to-it-iveness: He developed his idea for bringing colonists to Texas in response to a national recession that had forced his business into bankruptcy. Moses personally appeared before the Spanish governor in San Antonio to make a case for his proposal—and he succeeded!

Moses' refusal to give up and his ability to get others to buy into his ideas really struck a chord with me. They reminded me of some of the challenges I faced during my journey with The Bell Tower on 34th, challenges I'll tell you about later in this book.

Unfortunately, Moses' health gave out before he realized his goal. After Moses died in June 1821, Stephen stepped up to finish the work his father started. And like his father, Stephen demonstrated dogged determination to keep on going in the face of considerable challenges. Stephen negotiated with the Mexican government (which had recently won its independence from Spain) to bring 300 settlers to Mexico's province of Texas.

After getting permission to proceed, Stephen began getting the word out about his intention to settle southeast and central Texas. The opportunity to buy inexpensive Texas land (it cost considerably less than U.S. public lands) was an enticing one, and interested buyers started streaming into Texas from throughout America, particularly from Louisiana, Alabama, Arkansas, Tennessee, and Missouri.

That was a victory, but it also presented further challenges for Stephen. He was responsible not only for awarding land grants, but also for helping the settlers succeed. He also protected them from hostile native Americans and helped them find food. Stephen never stopped persevering, and as a result, his colonies were, indeed, successful. His dedication made the Texas we know today possible.

ANOTHER FATHER AND SON: THE MORTONS

One of those to jump at the opportunity in Texas was farmer William P. Morton, the man named on the 1824 land grant I received. Of course, I couldn't resist researching his story. What I found was another example of stick-to-itiveness.

William sailed the Gulf of Mexico to Texas from Mobile, Alabama, in 1822 with his wife and five children. The trip went smoothly until the family reached the island of Galveston, southeast of Houston. Then they wrecked their boat off Galveston's coast and found themselves stranded there.

William and his 17-year-old son, John, rowed a piece of wreckage west along the coast until they found the mouth of the Brazos River, two miles south of present-day Freeport. Imagine it: they rowed approximately 36 nautical miles.

Once they started making their way up the Brazos, William and John encountered another group of Texas colonists-to-be: passengers of *The Lively* from New Orleans. They helped William and John build a small boat, making it possible for them to make their way back to Galveston to get the rest of their family.

The Mortons did eventually meet with Stephen F. Austin. William became one of Stephen's first settlers, who also are known as "Austin's 300."

William's determination paid off for him and his family. On July 15, 1824, William was granted 1½ leagues of land (one league is 4428.4 acres of grazing land) along with one labor (177.1 acres of cropland) in what is now Fort Bend County, southwest of Houston.

A BIT OF MYSTERY

One thing that puzzled me as I reviewed my 1824 land grant documents was how a grant for land in Fort Bend County could be linked with our Houston property, property that was more than 30 miles away in another county. After spending more time reviewing my documents, and continued research, I think I found my answer…or at least a partial answer.

I'm fairly confident that my property documents

refer to two William P. Mortons: father and son, though there are no references to a "senior" or a "junior." I believe it was the father who received the 1824 land grant I've described, via Stephen F. Austin, for property along the Brazos River. The son later received a land grant of

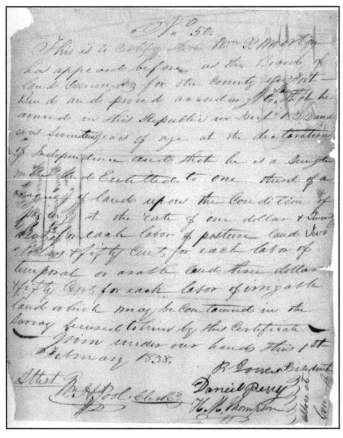

Part of the 1836 document that certifies the younger William P. Morton qualified for a one-third league land grant from the Republic of Texas.

his own, from the Republic of Texas, for property in Harris County.

I was able to find genealogical records that confirm the existence of a father and son, both named William P. Morton. And after closer review of my own documents, I realized the handwritten portion includes pages from an 1845 land grant from the Republic of Mexico to William P. Morton. The 1845 grant states:

"I, Anson Jones, President of the Republic aforesaid (Jones was the Texas president from 1844 to 1846), by virtue of the power vested in me by Law and In accordance with the Statutes of said Republic, in such case made and provided, do by these presents Grant to William P. Morton, his heirs or assigns forever One Third of a league acres of Land, situated and described as follows; in Harris County on White Oak Bayou a branch of Buffalo Bayou…"

Also interesting, I later discovered that the Texas Land Office has documentation from 1836 stating that William P. Morton met the legal standard for a Republic of Texas headright land grant.

"This is to certify that Mr. William P. Morton has appeared before this board of land commissioners for the County of Fort Bend and provided according to the law that he arrived in this Republic in [illegible] in 1822 and was 17 years of age at the Declaration of Independence and that

he is a single man and entitled to one third of a
league of land upon the condition of payment..."

This statement provides more evidence that it was a
younger William P. Morton who received the one-third
league grant where our venue now operates. The elder
William P. Morton was in his 40s and already the father
of five when he brought his family to the province of
Texas in 1822. And that was 14 years before the Texas
Declaration of Independence was signed.

The headright land grants, by the way, were provided
for in the Republic of Texas' 1836 constitution. It stated
that all single men age 17 and older who lived in Texas
when the Texas Declaration of Independence was
signed (March 4, 1836) would receive one-third of a
league of land.

That statement explains why the Republic of Texas
certified that William was 17 when the Declaration of
Independence was signed and that he was single.

I've only been able to find a few more details about
the life of the younger William P. Morton. In 1836, he
was awarded his portion of the family estate in Fort
Bend County: 1,384 acres.

There's also a record of him buying slaves in
Brazoria County in 1844, shortly before becoming
owner of the one-third league. The records show he paid
$1,000 for "Big Ned," age 22, and "Little Ned," with no
age information.

I do know, based on 1830s-era maps of the area, that
the land William acquired was heavily wooded. He may

have planned to rely on slave labor to establish and work his farm.

I'm still not completely sure why the documents that my title search yielded would include a grant to land other than my own. It could be that the title company researched the name of the second grant holder, William P. Morton, and simply included all of the land records they had with his name. They might have assumed everything they provided pertained to one man, not a father and son.

NEIGHBORS OF NOTE

As I started studying the land grants surrounding the younger William Morton's one-third league in Harris County, I realized that William had a pretty impressive neighbor. The land sat just northwest of two leagues owned by John Austin—another one of Austin's 300.

John's land would play a vital role in the history of Texas.

After John died of cholera in 1833, his wife, Elizabeth Austin, inherited his tract. She and her second husband, Thomas F.L. Parrot, went on to sell the southern portion to brothers Augustus and John Allen, who by the way, were extremely determined—and one could argue, brazen. The brothers felt the land's proximity to Buffalo Bayou made it an ideal spot to develop a town. They named their new development Houston and successfully lobbied to make it the capital of the new Texas republic. When marketing Houston, the Allen brothers wrote there was "no place in Texas more healthy, having an abundance of excellent spring water, and enjoying the sea breeze in all its freshness." Never mind the fact that Houston was 50 miles away from the ocean and far from the ideal setting the brothers described.

"Everything about the land was wild, savage and uncontrollable," writes Jim Henderson in his book, *Houston: A History of a Giant.* "The rains and the heat were merciless; rivers often swelled over their banks and washed across the defenseless countryside; Gulf storms pulled trees from the ground by the roots and assaulted the coast with tidal waves."

The brothers' grit and bold courage paid off. Houston was the Texas state capital until yellow fever epidemics led Texas lawmakers to select Austin as the new capital in 1838. It remained one of the state's most important cities, and today, as I mentioned, Houston is the fourth-largest city in the country.

John Austin played an important role in Texas history, too. According to the Texas State Historical Association, he possibly was a distant relative of Stephen F. Austin himself. If they weren't related, John and Stephen definitely were close friends. John had opened a mercantile store with J.E.B. Austin, Stephen's brother, in the 1820s. John also had business interests in cattle, shipping, and a cotton gin on Buffalo Bayou. During the Texas Revolution, he led at the Battle of Velasco and later served as the militia's brigadier general.

Austin wasn't the younger William Morton's only interesting neighbor. Another, Johann Gerhard Reinermann, was among the first German immigrants to settle in western Harris County. As you'll soon see, their story would intertwine with those of future Morton tract property owners.

The Republic of Texas awarded a league to Johann's family in 1838, after Johann's death, and his son, Henry Reinermann, received a one-third league headright grant immediately above it. The William Morton one-third league sat immediately above Henry's land.

GERMAN SETTLERS

Because some of the handwritten documents my title search yielded are difficult to read, and possibly incomplete, I can't tell when William P. Morton sold the one-third league he acquired from the Republic of Texas.

But, I do have a somewhat complete chain of owners from the 1860s until I became the owner roughly 150 years later.

One significant link in that chain is Henry Vollmer, Sr., who paid $150 for 25 acres of the William P. Morton one-third league on Nov. 25, 1865. It appears that Henry (1821-1878), his wife, Katherine (Fenger) Ojemann (1820-1895), and their children went on to be important members of their community, a small settlement of German immigrants.

Their village, which included the land where The Bell Tower on 34th now is, comprised scattered farms surrounded by still heavily wooded land. The village actually was originally named Vollmer—for the Vollmer family—although it was later re-named White Oak after the nearby bayou.

According to an article in *Absolutely Memorial* magazine, the land along White Oak Bayou, a mix of clay and sand, was fertile and available for 50 cents per acre, making it an attractive deal for settlers who wanted to establish farms there.

"Today, this area is well within (Houston) city limits..., but in the 1860s, these communities were quite distant from urban Houston," says the article, which was contributed by The Heritage Society, a Houston-based preservation organization.

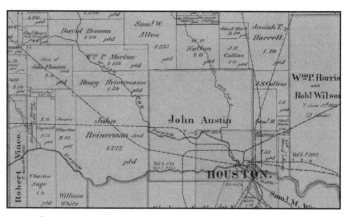

This 19th Century Harris County map shows the William P. Morton land grant, along with the property owned by the Reinermans and the John Austin land grant. Pressler, Herman. Map of Harris County, 1896. Map 4675, Map Collection, Archives and Records Program, Texas General Land Office, Austin, TX.

Dan Worrall mentions the Vollmer/White Oak community in his 2016 history book, *Pleasant Bend: Upper Buffalo Bayou and the San Felipe Trail in the Nineteenth Century.*

The book says Vollmer/White Oak had its own post office, and in 1873, the White Oak Schuetzen Verein (gun club) organized on what is now Mangum Manor Park on Saxon Drive. At the time, Schuetzen Verein was considered one of the finest of Harris County's many gun clubs. These organizations hosted picnics, dances, and shooting competitions with other clubs, Dan Worrall writes, which promoted close ties among the small German communities in the area.

Dan Worrall's book actually shows the land where The Bell Tower on 34th now is on an 1891 map of the White Oak community. Immediately to the north of what is now my property was the White Oak School. And north of the school was St. John Evangelical Lutheran Church. Both were along what is now Mangum Road.

The Vollmers are mentioned in the *Pleasant Bend* book, too. When they settled in Harris County, Henry Vollmer bought a 100-acre east-west elongated strip of land near the top of the Johann Reinermann league, where he built a house.

Here's the part of the book that excited me: "Henry prospered with his farm, and he invested in more land. This land went to his children...Son John Vollmer received a piece on *the Morton tract.*"

Somehow, finding the Morton tract and the Vollmers

in this book, a source in addition to the title documents, made my land's story seem more real, more three-dimensional to me. It was an exhilarating moment.

Not only do the Vollmers represent a link between our business and Texas history, they also stand out as another example of people who demonstrated great fortitude. German settlers in west and northwest Harris County coped with sweltering heat, prairie fires, and devastating floods. There was the risk of attack by bears, wild hogs and other wild animals; the threats of malaria and yellow fever; and the day-to-day challenges of working a farm. Not only did the Vollmers keep on going, they helped build a thriving community.

Though the White Oak area has been swallowed up by Houston, signs of the Vollmer family and their legacy remain. Vollmer Road, west of us in Houston's Spring Branch community, is a north-south road that forms a T-intersection on West 34th Street.

And south of us, about a 10-minute drive from The Bell Tower on 34th, is the Vollmer Cemetery. Henry Vollmer Sr. and his wife and children are buried there.

Glimpses of the Vollmer's community remain, too. St. John Evangelical Lutheran Church, which was founded in the 1860s and rebuilt in 1891, was moved out of the White Oak area in 1968 by the Heritage Society. In its new location, Sam Houston Park in downtown Houston, the church is open to public tours as a historical building.

You also can see a historical marker at 4606 Mangum Road—about 4 ½ miles from The Bell Tower

St John Evangelical Lutheran Church, built by the Vollmer/ White Oak community, in its current, downtown Houston location. From the Collections of The Heritage Society, Houston, Texas.

on 34th—to commemorate the church's original location in White Oak.

Though I attempted to research all of the families who've owned portions of the Morton one-third league over the years, I haven't been able to find as many details about them. But I've recognized the names of Henry and Kate's children and grandchildren on title documents. Those names include sons John Vollmer (1855-1935) and William Vollmer (1862-1940). They also include the children of William and Annie Vollmer: Paul Vollmer (1903-1963) and wife Dena Vollmer, along with Kate Vollmer Niemann (1889-1939) and husband Henry Niemann (1853-1938).

Based on their names, many of the other Morton tract land owners over the years probably were of German descent, too. Those names include Beneke, Brandt, Eikemeyer, Kuehn, Lange, Paschen, Prause, Schaper, Struebing, and Wigelow.

After exploring our property's ties to early Texas history, and our community's German heritage, I discovered equally fascinating stories about the people, businesses, and events that took place in the 20th century.

Bell Tower Trivia

WILLIAM P. MORTON, THE MAN NAMED
ON THE 1824 LAND GRANT I RECEIVED,
IS BELIEVED TO HAVE DROWNED WHEN
THE BRAZOS RIVER FLOODED IN 1833.
IN FEBRUARY 1836, HIS WIDOW SOLD
A PORTION OF HIS LAND TO ROBERT
EDEN HANDY AND WILLIAM LUSK,
WHO WENT ON TO DEVELOP THE
CITY OF RICHMOND, TEXAS THERE.
WHEN FORT BEND COUNTY WAS
FORMED, RICHMOND BECAME ITS SEAT
OF GOVERNMENT.

Chapter 3

THE NOT-SO-DISTANT PAST

THE AREA SURROUNDING OUR PROPERTY started seeing major transformations in the 1900s. One of the most significant changes was the development of Garden Oaks, a neighborhood established by Houston businessman Edward Lilo (E.L.) Crain in 1937. E.L. (1885-1950) designed Garden Oaks in hopes of creating a "Small town, USA" in Houston, according to local historian Marks Hinton, author of *Historic Houston Streets: The Stories Behind the Names.*

E.L. incorporated winding streets into his new neighborhood, along with over-sized lots shaded by large trees. Each homebuyer received a crape myrtle tree and rose bushes when they moved in. Within 10 years,

Garden Oaks was popular with middle class families and newly returned World War II veterans who had the assistance of the 1944 G.I. Bill to make their purchases.

E.L. was a true visionary. His Houston-based business, Crain Ready-Cut House Company, manufactured thousands of pre-fabricated houses in the 1920s. The company saw tremendous success when E.L. merged home manufacturing with neighborhood development: He created communities, including Houston's Avondale Neighborhood and Southside Place, and filled them with his company's houses.

When the Great Depression cut into demand for new houses, E.L. didn't give up. His company found alternative construction projects, including a portable ice cream parlor and a portable short-order restaurant.

The passage of the Federal Housing Act paved the way for the most ambitious project of E.L.'s career: the Garden Oaks development. Four years after E.L. purchased 750 acres for his project, he'd platted 1,150 building lots, created parks and playgrounds, and built 681 houses. Clearly, tenacity and vision won the day for E.L. Crain—and resulted in the beautiful neighborhood that The Bell Tower on 34th now calls home.

THE DANCE HALL YEARS

Although my future property was gaining some residential and commercial neighbors, it still was mostly rural when it caught the eye of Willie Henry "Bill" Mraz in the late 1940s.

Willie H. (Bill) Mraz
Shiner, Texas
2.3.07 - 11.27.75

Bill Mraz in his youth.
Photo courtesy of the Texas
Historical Commission.

Bill (1907-1975) was born and raised in the farming community of Moulton, Texas, between Houston and San Antonio. His parents were part of a large population of Czech immigrants in the area. In the 1920s, after marrying Anna Motl in nearby Shiner, Bill relocated to Houston. There, he found work as a bricklayer and opportunities to pursue one of his greatest loves: polka music. He started by playing accordion with his brother, Mills, at house parties, and later formed his own polka band.

Bill was standing on the grounds of the Miller Dance Hall on Rosslyn Road (later 34th Street), when he noticed a barn for sale across the way—at the site that would one day become The Bell Tower on 34th. The Bill Mraz Orchestra had been popular at the Miller Dance Hall since 1936, and Bill's success allowed him to buy the venue in 1945. His business thrived—it started struggling to hold the large crowds it was drawing. The barn across the street and the land around might have needed some work, but that didn't discourage him in the least. To Bill, the barn was a business opportunity.

He snapped up the property and, shortly after, announced plans to build a new dance hall on about three acres of "more spacious and beautiful grounds."

Construction on the new facility began in February 1948. "We're going to have the largest floor in town, 9,500 square feet, made of the finest maple flooring," Bill announced at the time. The dance hall and barbecue joint opened on Aug. 15, 1948. That night, the hall collected 4,527 tickets, and even more people stood outside to hear the music of the Bill Mraz Orchestra.

Bill's granddaughter, Stephanie Janda, described the business' early success during a 2004 interview with the *Houston Chronicle*. "It was just packed," she said. "People would come out here day after day. They would bring their kids and leave their cares behind."

From that point on, it was full steam ahead for Bill and the dance hall. He may not have used the words "keep on going," but he certainly exemplified them as he built his business. Before long, people were calling his dance hall the "Polka Capital of Texas," and the venue was attracting big names in polka music including Frankie Yankovic, Eddie Skeets and The Six Fat Dutchman, among others.

Until 1950, our future property was just outside Houston city limits: it was considered part of unincorporated Harris County. After Houston expanded its city limits and annexed the dance hall property, Bill and Anna successfully petitioned City Council to waive

People lined up at the door to get in Bill Mraz Dance Hall on its opening night in 1948. Source: Texas Historical Commission.

The crowd inside the Bill Mraz Dance Hall on a Saturday night in the 1950s. Source: Texas Historical Commission.

fire hazard requirements for their occupancy permit because the hall was larger than typical recreation facilities under city code at the time.

In 1954, Bill built a house for himself and Anna, followed by houses for sons Eugene and Rudy in 1961 and 1966. The family also built two buildings available for commercial lease. Their first tenants included a barber shop and a dry cleaner. And later, after the family expanded the commercial properties, a small shop and metal warehouse facility moved in. Most of those buildings remain on our property today; we use them for storage.

By 1965, steadily growing crowds led Bill to expand the dance hall, bringing it to 11,000 square feet. The lime green and white (later changed to red with white trim) building remained a magnet for area audiences.

In addition to throwing square dancing and all-day polka dances known as polka jamborees, the venue was presenting live radio shows. In fact, Bill hosted a polka radio show on KFRD in Rosenberg (southwest of Houston) for years.

Bill's barbecue was a hit, too. He served it at private parties around town and during his polka jamborees. For him, barbecuing was serious business. He custom designed his barbecue pit and created secret recipes for sauces, potato salad, and ranch style beans.

In addition to individual customers, the dance hall was a popular spot for private parties—a foreshadowing, maybe, of The Bell Tower on 34th. Tenneco, Gulf, Exxon, Century 21, and trail rider associations leased the hall. Houston mayors Louie Welch and Fred Hofheinz hosted campaign fundraisers there.

Bill's family continued to operate the dance hall until 1986, when financial difficulties forced them to close.

In November 1997, the hall was added to the National Register of Historic Places, and in February 1999, the City of Houston recognized the hall as a historical landmark.

Several years later, in 2002, Bill's family re-opened the dance hall's doors, attracting nearly 2,000 people on their first day back in business.

The business thrived until 2004 when a fire destroyed the hall, along with countless old photos and memorabilia inside. The fire was ruled an accident by the Houston Fire Department.

Though no one was hurt, the fire was a blow to the community and the dance hall's regulars.

During the venue's final years of business, its website described the dance hall's rich history. One of the keys to Bill Mraz's success over the years was his ability to help people connect with their culture and their community, the website said.

"At the Dance Hall, Bill provided an environment where for the Czech people and native music sung in the Czech language could be found. For German and Polish people, music with lyrics performed in their native language could be heard by visiting bands. For singles, the Dance Hall became a meeting and courting place.

The re-opening of the Bill Mraz Dance Hall generated a great deal of excitement within the community.

Fire destroyed the Bill Mraz Dance Hall in 2004.

Numerous traditional wedding receptions were held for couples that credited Bill's Dance Hall with their 'once in a lifetime' chance meeting. From that point forward, the couples brought their children. On any given night it was common to see tables and benches with homemade quilts beneath sleeping children. For people of the Houston Czech community like Bill and Anna that left their family farms, the Dance Hall re-created the Czech social environment their parents preserved in their small farming communities when they first came to Texas and brought some of this country environment into the bustling big city."

Bill was remembered fondly on the website, too.

"He was one of the first recipients of the prestigious Lifetime Achievement Awards given annually by the Texas Polka Music Association for his contributions to Czech polka music in Texas. Both Bill and his Dance Hall had become so well-known and well liked that when he died of a heart attack while working at his Bar-B-Q pit on November 22, 1975, Houston

Mayor Fred Hofheinz signed a proclamation making November 22, 1975, 'Bill Mraz Day.'" Even today, there is a Bill Mraz Ballroom Fan Club on Facebook. And as recently as 2014, The Texas Czech Heritage & Cultural Center honored Texas polka bands of the past, including Bill Mraz Orchestra. If Bill hadn't dreamed big, and pursued that dream with such determination, none of those things would have been possible.

LAST FEW OWNERS

For a while after the dance hall burned down, some of the Mraz family continued to live in houses on the property, before the property was sold to a commercial developer in 2007 named Titus Inc., the company owned by the businessman mentioned in this book's introduction.

From there, the land was transferred to bankruptcy trustees and an investment company before "Keep on Going," the company formed by my wife, Angela, and me, was able to buy it.

But long before we bought this property, I had a significant part to play in the unbelievable events that led to the establishment of The Bell Tower on 34th. For me, it was one of the most challenging chapters of my life.

Bell Tower Trivia

A MASON JAR CONTAINING $13,000
WAS ONCE FOUND BURIED AT THE
BASE OF AN OLD TREE ON THE VENUE'S
GROUNDS. IT PRESUMABLY WAS BURIED
BY BILL MRAZ OR HIS WIFE.

Chapter 4

THE STORM

THE POUNDING ON MY FRONT DOOR WAS getting louder and more insistent. And angrier, definitely angrier. If I'd been home alone, I might have spoken with the ill-tempered visitor at my door and tried to defuse what I knew was misdirected anger. But my wife and children were home, and there was a very real possibility that this situation could escalate into something dangerous. Instead, I left the knocks unanswered.

By that evening in fall 2008, I was the focus of hostility for so many people, from brides to waiters to construction workers, that I couldn't begin to count them. At first, they called me or approached me at my office, but more recently, they'd been attempting to confront me at home. A couple of men had even shown up with weapons, but thankfully, they left when no one responded to their knocks on the door.

As nerve-racking as this situation was, I understood the feelings of frustration, helplessness, and despair these people were experiencing. All of them, like me, had been caught in the wake of the broken promises of the wedding venue owner I told you about, his sudden disappearance with what we assumed to be hundreds of thousands of dollars in brides' deposits, and his abandoned facilities. His businesses wouldn't be hosting anyone's dream wedding that fall—or ever. And the scores of people who depended on this man's company for paychecks, or payments for labor and supplies they'd provided to build his newest venue, were out of luck.

Over time, the employees of the venue owner, Daniel Blasingame, dubbed him "Evil Dan," a name that my children and I also adopted and still use when referring to him.

I really couldn't blame people who'd been burned by Evil Dan for trying to break my door down, even though I was as much a victim as they were. As the general contractor responsible for the construction of Evil Dan's second Houston wedding venue, I was among those who'd suffered devastating financial loss at the hands of his company.

Unfortunately, because of my close association with Evil Dan and his company, people were assuming that I shared responsibility for their difficulties. My name and business were displayed on the "Coming Soon" sign at 835 W. 34th St., where the new wedding venue was being constructed. Even worse, when Evil Dan told brides and grooms-to-be about the fabulous new venue I was building for him during the last year, he described me as a partner. (In reality, I was falsely misled to believe I would have a 15 percent stake in the business, but that never came to fruition.)

In any case, people who'd been wronged by Evil Dan wanted their pound of flesh. And some of them were making threats, the kinds of threats that made me fear for my family's safety.

All of this was happening while my company, Igo Developments, spiraled into a dire financial situation. Evil Dan and his partners owed me more than $1.5 million, money I wouldn't be seeing. There was no bringing the company back from this.

My business and reputation were in ruins. My wife, Angela, was unhappy with me. I couldn't provide for my family. And, now, as a seemingly unending stream of angry brides, workers, and suppliers pursued me, it seemed I'd put my wife and our children in harm's way.

I didn't know what to do.

How was this mess even possible?

MEETING THE PRESIDENT'S BUTLER

Just one year earlier, I had every reason to be optimistic about my life and business.

My general contracting company, then only a few years old, had a full project load and a solid reputation for reliable, quality work. By that point in my career, I'd already worked as a professional saxophonist and band manager, a project manager and superintendent for a home builder, and a real estate broker. Each chapter in my professional journey had given me skills and knowledge that proved valuable in subsequent chapters.

MEET ROGER IGO

I HAVE BEEN DESCRIBED BY SOME AS A BUSInessman with soul.

That's because long before I was a CEO, or a general contractor or a realtor, I attended Berklee College of Music in Boston and earned most of my living playing saxophone.

Well, I was making ends meet. Money was tight. Back in the early days of my musical career, in the early '90s, my possessions totaled little more than two pairs of pants, my motorcycle, and, of course, my sax.

But as far as I was concerned, I was living the dream. I was a 20-something doing what I loved most. You could argue that even though I didn't think about it at the time, I was building experience doing a bit of what I now consider the core mission of The Bell Tower on 34th: delivering

*Here I am warming up for the
2017 Global Village reunion show.*

excellent events that no one will ever forget. After all, as an entertainer, my job was creating memorable moments for audiences in the form of standout performances.

Actually, you could argue that I started honing my customer service skills earlier than that. Much earlier. When I was about 5 ½ years old, I was finding work in my neighborhood, from weed pulling to washing dogs to trapping lizards—just about any kind of odd job you can imagine. I continued that work through high school, and by the time I graduated from Clements High School in 1989, I had quite a few regulars.

I delved into sales at an early age, too.

When I was about 8½, I started selling fudge door-to-door. And not long after that, I started earning extra money selling cold cans of Pepsi to construction workers and candy to my friends.

By the time I was 10, my older half-sister, Andrea, referred to me as an entrepreneur. That moment has always stuck with me. It was the first time I heard that word.

But Andrea was on to something. A couple of years later I started my own Sno-Cone business, Party Flavors on Ice.

After high school, my focus shifted to more steady forms of income, from sacking groceries to phone sales, so I could cover my music studies and supplement the money I was bringing in playing sax.

From 1990 to 1996, I played jazz and blues—and later funk—with a Houston-area band called Global Village.

Sometime during that period, I moved into the role of band manager while continuing to perform. In 1992, I helped establish World Records, our band's own recording label, and later founded Silverdome Publishing Company, which was supposed to issue licenses for the use of musicians' songs and collect royalties for them.

While I was managing the band, we distributed performance news for client musicians in the form of the Texas Funk Syndicate. It started as a postcard—this was before the Internet era—and I sold advertising space on it to clubs, bands, and promoters around town to pay for the printing and postage. Over time, the postcard grew, and eventually, evolved into a small newspaper.

I also concluded over time that business was a natural fit for me, and I started looking for other opportunities.

After a brief period in luxury home construction as a project manager, I went on to earn my real estate license and to study business law at Houston Community College.

I should mention that even though I left the music industry, the Global Village members and I stayed in touch. We even met for a reunion concert at The Bell Tower on 34th in December

2017. I can't tell you how great it felt to make music with my old friends again.

During my years in residential real estate, I founded Igo Properties, became a "Million Dollar Producer," and hosted *The New Home Radio Show* on KSEV 700 AM for listeners in Houston, Austin, and San Antonio.

Several years later, I made the shift from guiding clients through property sales and purchases to helping people build properties. I'd worked in construction before, but now I was doing it as an entrepreneur. My general contracting business, Igo Developments, got its start in roughly 2004.

I can't say that everything I touched was gold until my business dealings with Evil Dan, but overall, I was blessed with steady successes and healthy, growing businesses.

Perhaps one of the most important keys to my success has been the support of my family. My mom, for example, Trauma Resolution Therapist Eriko Valk, has been a constant sounding board, encourager, and prayer warrior on my behalf.

My wife, Angela, has stood by my side and offered invaluable insights through every trial and success.

One of my favorite pictures of Angela and me.

And even though the challenges I eventually faced were very hard on all my loved ones, their love was a critical lifeline for me during the dark times.

General contracting felt like a perfect fit. I loved managing all of the moving parts that go into a construction project. I saw the inevitable challenges that surface during large jobs as puzzles to be solved. And I loved the working relationships I developed with staff, subcontractors, and clients.

I thought my company, Igo Developments, was so successful that in 2008 I told Angela, who had a very successful career selling real estate advertising for the *Houston Chronicle* for 13 years, that she could leave her job. She was free, I told her, to focus on raising our children and painting works of art like she always wanted.

I couldn't have known that I was walking toward one of the most painful journeys of my life, or, that someone I loved and trusted would put me on that path. My business dealings with Evil Dan started with a simple introduction by my dad, Bob.

I should clarify that Bob was my step-father. My father, George Igo, has been an important part of my life since I was born, and we're still close today. But Bob was the head of the household when I was growing up. He helped raise me, and I loved him and called him Dad.

I also respected Bob, as many people did, for his success as a restaurateur. In fact, if he hadn't been so good at what he did, there's a good chance that neither of us would have crossed paths with Evil Dan.

By the time Bob died of liver disease at age 66 in May 2015, he had been a restaurateur for more than 40 years. One of his greatest claims to fame was his role in developing one of Houston's most important Tex-Mex staples, next to chips and salsa: machine-made frozen margaritas.

FAMILY LEGEND

BOB'S CAREER AS A RESTAURATEUR IS legend in our family. It started when Bob was a college dropout working the loading docks along the Houston Ship Channel and completely unsure of the path he wanted to take in life.

He once told me that at some point he'd saved up enough money to buy himself a steak dinner. At a local restaurant that night, Bob noticed that a group of customers had left a waiter a $5 tip. This was the early '70s. That was a big tip. And the steakhouse, it was air conditioned, unlike the loading docks.

That's when Bob realized he wanted to work in restaurants. He got his start as a bartender and advanced to bar manager. And eventually, he started working for Houston's Garbett family, founder of the Los Tios restaurant chain. At the time, Los Tios was synonymous with Tex-Mex food in Houston.

It was the Garbett family who sent Bob to the Texas State Fair with the company charge card to research the latest and greatest in 1970s food trends.

My second dad, Bob.

Bob returned with a soft-serve ice cream machine manufactured by Lane Equipment Company. The Garbetts were less than enthusiastic about the purchase that had been made with their money. In fact, Bob almost lost his job.

But Bob wasn't planning to add ice cream to Los Tios' menu. I'm not sure what inspired him, but with the understanding that tequila never freezes, Bob was envisioning a soft-serve ice cream machine that dispensed the slushy goodness that we know today as frozen margaritas. They were a considerable change from the blender-made margaritas available then—that process was noisy and inefficient.

It didn't take long for Bob's new approach to margarita-making to catch on at Los Tios, and at restaurants throughout the city. (Controversially, about the same time or soon after, there was another man in Dallas, Texas, who also claims to have originated the idea, and he promoted it more aggressively.)

Over the years, Bob went on to consult for and work for such well-known Houston restaurant concepts as Strawberry Patch, Mason Jar, and Guadalajara. He also started or co-owned restaurants of his own. Two of them, Fajita Flats and Live Oak Grill, remain in business today under different ownership. Another, Hill Country Pasta House, recently closed.

During the last 10-15 years of his life, Bob was a sought-after restaurant consultant in Houston and the surrounding region.

That's how Evil Dan heard about him. In the mid-2000s, Evil Dan was in a dispute with his landlord, the man who owned the building where Evil Dan's company, Titus Inc., operated Bella Terrazza.

I don't know the details, only that Evil Dan apparently thought Bob's restaurant and business expertise would be relevant to his landlord dispute, and so Evil

Dan asked Bob to serve as a mediator. After Bob successfully helped Titus and their landlord come to an acceptable resolution, Evil Dan started seeking Bob's advice on additional matters. Over time, Evil Dan invited Bob to take an even larger role with Titus, and Bob eventually became a one-third owner of the company with Evil Dan and his mother. After that, when Titus applied for bank loans, it had Bob's good name, not to mention his strong credit and his assets, to make the application stronger.

It doesn't appear that Bob benefited significantly from this business relationship. I think that he, like many people, was drawn in by Evil Dan's charisma and his apparent business know-how. Maybe Bob saw being part of Titus as a positive career development.

I can empathize with Bob's response to Evil Dan. When Bob introduced us, Evil Dan won me over, too.

I don't remember exactly when I met the man we now think of as Evil Dan. What I do remember is that moments after shaking hands, out of the blue he explained how he'd once been President George H.W. Bush's butler. This man had an almost theatrical quality and was a master storyteller. And his stories were so over the top that *they had to be true.* How could you say you've been George Bush's butler? It was a big enough story that you had to believe it. In hindsight, the butler story should have been more of a red flag than something to admire. But at the time I thought, wow, this guy's big time. How did Bob get a chance to own part of this business?

So, when Bob encouraged me to bid on Titus' newest construction project, I bought into the vision. I was of the mindset that I'd be taking my company to a new level...and I would be helping a project that was important to the success of my step-dad's company.

BETRAYALS

I was truly excited about the opportunity to bid on Titus' project: the construction of a second local wedding venue. Actually, the building was really more of a replacement than a new location. Titus' existing venue, Bella Terrazza, was a bougainvillea-covered Old World-style villa based in Houston's upscale Galleria area. From all appearances, business was good. Titus also owned the venue's successful in-house catering service, Chef's Table.

It was explained to me that Titus at the time was nearing the end of a 10-year lease with Bella Terrazza's landlord and was ready for a change. After some time the company had selected 3.2 acres of land in northwest Houston, the former home of Houston's legendary Bill Mraz Dance Hall, for a new venture called The Tuscany of Garden Oaks. Once the new wedding and events venue was up and running, Titus planned to shutter Bella Terrazza permanently if they could not reach a new lease agreement with their landlord.

The Tuscany of Garden Oaks was to be a lavish, Mediterranean-style event venue spanning more than 33,000 square feet. Initial building plans included a chapel, wine cellar, even ceilings painted to resemble those in the famed Sistine Chapel.

Out of all of the factors that sold me on Titus' project, Bob's involvement carried the most weight in my mind. Looking back, I see that the Titus leadership team used my love and trust for Bob to their advantage. In September 2006, they made me believe that as Bob's son, I would be receiving 15 percent ownership of Titus Inc. in the form of company shares along with annual dividend payments—all as a result of Bob's generous investment in the company. I assume they thought that if I had a vested interest in the company's success, I'd be more likely to support their efforts to buy land and build a new venue on it. And they were right.

Bob's partners gave me a stock certificate and $2,500 in cash, which was supposed to be the first of my dividend payments. I thanked them and didn't look at the stock certificate again until more than a year later. That's when I realized the exact wording was "one hundred and fifty shares of common stock" out of a million shares. What that meant was I didn't receive 15 percent company ownership—it only was .015 percent: less than one-eighth of 1 percent.

I wish I'd realized that before I agreed to loan Titus Inc. $100,000 to facilitate their purchase of the property on West 34th Street. I even agreed to charge zero interest unless they defaulted. The note was supposed to be secured by a promissory note for an additional 10 percent ownership of the future event venue. It was signed by one of Bob's other Titus Inc. partners, Evil Dan's mother.

The first payment on the loan was $25,000, which I received on Dec. 11, 2006. That was it. I would never receive any additional payments for the $100,000 loan or ownership in the new venue.

But, of course, hindsight is 20-20. Back in late 2006 and early 2007, I was still happy to do as much as I could to help one of Bob's companies with its new venture.

When Titus bought the land on West 34th Street, I served as Titus' agent. For the property closing, I wired $25,000 to the title company for Titus. I also agreed to give—or more accurately, was tricked into giving—my $27,500 real estate commission to them so they could put it toward closing costs. There wasn't even talk of paying me back. Not only that, Titus didn't have any funds for their option fee. Against my better judgment, I used a check from my credit card provider to provide Titus another $10,000 so they could pay the fee.

By the time the closing was complete, I had either loaned or given Titus a total of $137,500 on the premise that if the deal went through, this company that Bob had invested in might consider selecting me as their contractor to build their new facility.

Let's put it another way: I paid 44 percent of the buyer's closing costs, and Titus relied on loans from me to pay another 46 percent of them. That's 90 percent. And like I said, though I didn't know it, I owned less than one-eighth of 1 percent of Titus at the time.

I never received any other loan payments. I never received any additional shares of stock. I never received any more dividends. As for the $2,500 I received with my stock certificate, I obviously loaned Titus a far, far greater amount.

My blind faith and trust in Bob and his business partners kept me from seeing the writing on the wall.

What was to come, I was not prepared for, to say the least.

In March 2007 I received what I thought was good news: Titus decided to hire me as their general contractor. When they asked me to reduce the contract amount by removing my $80,000 builder's fee, I didn't see that as an unreasonable request. Titus explained that Bob had already started talking with a bank about a construction loan, and the amount did not include my builder's fee. Titus would still pay it, they said, over a 10-month period. Those $8,000 payments would be in addition to Titus' loan payments to me.

I don't know how they did it, but Titus did manage to pay me six out of the expected 10 monthly checks for the builder's fee. In the end, though, they only paid $48,000 of the promised $80,000. Throughout it all, even when I stopped receiving builder's fee installments, I continued to make progress on the project because I trusted and believed in Bob.

When I reflect now on the period when I worked for Evil Dan and Titus Inc., I think of the parable about a frog's response to hot water. The story goes that if you were to drop a frog in a pot of boiling water that it, naturally, would jump out to escape the sudden heat and pain. But if you were to put the frog in a comfy bath of room temperature water, and then heated the water gradually, the frog would be oblivious to the changes and stay put while you slowly boiled it to death.

I think that's what happened to me, and to Bob, and Evil Dan's employees. We were all frogs. At first, the water seemed fine. We had no idea that things were going to be getting considerably hotter.

QUEST FOR CANTERA AND THE DOOR MAN

ONE OF MY GREATEST—AND MOST POSitive—"adventures" with Evil Dan was our trip to central Mexico in search of Cantera stone.

Cantera, a light, durable volcanic rock, is mined only in certain regions of Mexico and Central America. The stone is easily carved, and its texture and flecks of color are stunning. Evil Dan was determined to incorporate it into practically every room in his new wedding venue. The plan was to find large quantities of Cantera stone, buy it, and have it shipped to the construction site in Houston.

We'd heard of a village named Morelia, in the state of Michoacán, where the surrounding mountains were covered with Cantera. So, in

June 2007 we flew into the closest major city, Guadalajara, to begin our quest. We traveled there with one of Evil Dan's employees, a waiter named Sergio Ruiz who agreed to join us as a guide and translator. And we rented a car. A car, as luck would have it, with no air conditioning.

Our first stop was the town of Tlaquepaque, in the state of Jalisco. The town is known for its colonial-era churches and mansions, and for its lush greenery, flowers, and orange trees. After checking in with the Chamber of Commerce, we were referred to Erich Wunsche Fierro, owner of Sebastian Exportaciones. Erich founded his company in 1987 to help Jalisco artisans sell their products abroad. Over time, it grew into a major exporter of handicrafts, decoration, and construction materials.

And Erich, Erich was practically the town mayor. After we met, it became abundantly clear that this was a man who'd earned the respect of his community. When Erich took us on a tour of Tlaquepaque, everywhere we stopped there seemed to be admirers, from tile manufacturers to pottery shops, rushing forward with warm greetings.

Among the places Erich took us was a tiny shop on the main street of town. It was hard to imagine it carrying much of an inventory, but Erich quickly led us out the back door to a massive field. It looked like farmland. Except the land was covered, as far as the eye could see, with a crop of giant metal chandeliers. We selected the largest one we could find and arranged for Erich to ship it to us.

Our new chandelier was about 13 feet tall and 11 feet wide. We later would have it cut into three pieces so it could fit through a giant window opening of the new venue, where it was reassembled and hung.

During our time with Erich, we went on to find tables, armoires, antique door knobs, and other decorative pieces that would enhance the new venue's atmosphere. By the end of our dealings together, Erich and I were friends. In fact, we remain in touch today.

As we continued on to Morelia, we started to notice roadside vendors selling Cantera stone and items made from it. One stretch had so many items that we decided to turn around and check it out. That's how we met our next guide on our journey: an older man named Rudolfo who, with his family, made a living from getting Cantera stone from the mountains, and selling columns, balustrades, and similar items made from it. As we became acquainted, we learned that Rudolfo knew Erich as well. The man offered to show us around, which resulted in hours of visits to roadside collections of his merchandise.

We were impressed, but were intent on going to "the source," the mountains, to get our Cantera stone.

So, we journeyed on in the oppressive summer heat in our car with no AC and made it to Morelia. We asked several people to take us to the nearest mountain before we finally realized that simply wasn't going to happen. Apparently, to visitors like us, the mountain was off limits. I am not exactly sure how, but apparently part of the mountain belonged to the village, and the people of Morelia guarded it and protected it as their private treasure. For us, there was no way to access the side of the mountain where the villagers were pulling out boulders.

At the same time, Morelia was covered in Cantera. It was under our feet, on the walls, overhead—everywhere we looked and just outside of our grasp.

Morelia also is filled with history: churches and Old World-style structures you might see in Spain or Italy.

We never did find what we were seeking in Morelia, but I was influenced by the architecture we saw there, the shapes of things and the carved stone. I hope to return one day.

But at that time, we concluded that our best source of Cantera stone was Rudolfo, the older man with the roadside merchandise. In the end, we made our purchases from him: Cantera stone for walls, floors, columns, balustrades...you name it.

Before we left the region, we shifted our focus to another potential local treasure: hand-carved wooden doors. Everyone we spoke to talked about a gifted man who made heavy, Old World-style doors with intricate carvings. We had to see him.

According to the people who recommended this talented door man, he was just "a little further down the road." I speak Spanish very well, but I never could get an exact address. So, Evil Dan and I left Morelia early one morning, a couple of white guys and a translator, and began our new quest. We clearly were outsiders and isolated. I can't say I always felt safe.

After a while, the road we were following shifted from a mostly straight trajectory to a more curvy, winding path. Dusk had fallen, and we had no idea if we were in the right spot or even close to the door man.

I didn't think about it at the time, but we literally were in a situation where we made a decision to "keep on going," and it paid off. After a long and exhausting drive, we found the workshop of a man who could help us, the perfect man for the job. He listened to us describe our venue project, and accepted an invitation to be flown to Houston to see our construction site. There, he took measurements of the door frames and made templates that he used to create heavy, beautifully carved doors for us. His handiwork was so heavy that we had to order special hinges for those doors. But the extra expense, and the journey, were well worth the gorgeous pieces the door man created for us, doors that still generate compliments and questions today.

So, all in all, our quest was a success. And I'm grateful for the opportunity I had to see so much Old World architecture. It really helped imprint in my mind's eye what the project was going to become. Make no mistake, the venue on 34th Street is nothing like the structures we saw in central Mexico, but seeing those historic buildings did inspire me. It broadened the horizon of opportunities for the project.

THE WATER SIMMERS

After Titus awarded Igo Developments the contract to serve as their new wedding venue's general contractor, the three Titus Inc. partners, including Bob, signed the standard construction loan documents. Normally, a performance bond would be required to make sure that subcontractors, laborers, and material suppliers were paid. But because Titus Inc. and I agreed to work with a funds management company, the performance bond requirement was waived. My company had lost its safety net, and I didn't even realize how desperately we needed it. I can't tell you how much I agonized over that turn of events later, even though I had no way of knowing how much peril my company, people, and suppliers were in at the time.

There would be more irregularities after construction got under way. Take the system that Titus put in place for covering the costs of materials and the subcontractors' work. Normally, general contractors make sure those expenses are covered by making periodic "draw requests" to the bank that's providing the project's construction loan. Titus said no: I had to send my draw requests to them. They would approach the bank and release checks for the subcontractors and suppliers for me to distribute.

The first three draws went smoothly.

Then, everything fell apart. It wasn't obvious at first, but the water in the pot had gotten much, much hotter.

In November 2007, Titus' bank stopped approving allocations. Evil Dan assured me that he would resolve the situation quickly. He was lying. I raised my concerns during daily conversations with Bob. Nothing changed.

I later learned—and documented to the best of my ability—that Titus had grossly misused funds totaling about $600,000 that should have covered construction costs.

I had no way of knowing that at the time. I saw the halt in funding as a temporary situation. That's what Titus called it. I focused on protecting the people I was responsible for until the situation was resolved. If taking care of them involved sacrificing my own well-being, so be it.

I started tapping into my own funds, borrowing against my company's lines of credit, and asking for personal favors. All I could think was that I had to get this project completed. Titus promised me that resolution to the bank situation was "just around the corner." It wasn't even in the same hemisphere.

Between November 2007 and May 2008, construction continued, but only because I was making it possible. I was led to believe by Bob and his partners that I would be given an additional 10 percent ownership of the business if I would just agree to continue the project using my own resources, which I did.

By May of 2008, the total owed to me and my subcontractors now totaled $1,240,903.

About a month later, things appeared to be looking

up. First of all, Titus' project was nearing Temporary Certificate of Occupancy status. The building wasn't officially complete, but Titus would be able to start holding events there in June 2008, as I'd promised. I'd actually promised a June 1 delivery, but I was not able to deliver until three days later. I felt good about coming so close to the promise date, despite the non-help of scheduled bank draws that were supposed to have materialized. Since the end of the project was getting close, and events were about to start, I had no reason to think I was not going to get the remaining money owed to me.

A couple of weeks later, I received what I thought was another promising sign. Bob asked me to meet him at Titus Inc.'s bank. I was going to receive a small, but very much needed payment of $100,000. All they needed was my signature.

The document the bank presented had three stipulations: I was waiving my right to sue Titus Inc.'s bank; I was not under duress; and I'd had ample time to consult an attorney.

I told Bob I felt uncomfortable signing a document like that, that I was tired and stressed and wanted time for my lawyer to see it. Bob's response? "Just sign it."

In the end, that's what I did. I trusted Bob.

I didn't know it, but I'd been betrayed. Again. It was one more painful truth I'd discover long after this: By agreeing not to sue their bank I'd left myself with no real recourse to fight for the money owed to me.

At the time, I clung to the hope that things had to

get better soon and continued to carry the increasingly heavy burden of keeping the project moving so we could finally finish the building. And it wasn't just me who was feeling that heat. I spent most of July and August 2008 talking down subcontractors and suppliers, trying to make them understand that I was waiting for the client to get more money from the bank. Many had been waiting since November 2007 to get paid for work or materials provided. They were hurting. And I was plagued by guilt and anxiety.

The situation only got worse. It didn't take long for me to exhaust my cash reserves and max out my personal financial resources. I was trying to buy time for Evil Dan's company for Bob's sake. I was trying to save my relationships with the suppliers and subcontractors. And no one was trying to do right by me.

By August 2008, my family needed money for back to school clothes and school supplies, money that I couldn't provide. Using my money to keep the construction on track was about to hurt my family. Now I was angry. Maybe furious would be a better word. Not to mention panicked. And desperate.

So, I tried to turn up the pressure: I filed a lien of more than $1.5 million—the total for months of unpaid subcontractor and supplier invoices—in hopes of forcing Titus' hand.

But my last-ditch effort just didn't work. At that point, I didn't know what to do. And things were about to heat up even more.

IKE BLOWS INTO TOWN

At 2:10 a.m. local time September 13, 2008, Hurricane Ike struck the Galveston coast, bringing with it a wall of water more than 13 feet high. With sustained winds of nearly 110 miles per hour, Ike was considered just one mile per hour short of a Category 3 hurricane. The hurricane relentlessly pummeled the Houston-Galveston area, and when it was done, 74 Texans had been killed. The storm left millions of people without power, some for weeks, and thousands without homes. Damage to the area was estimated at $29 million.

As for Titus' existing wedding venue, Bella Terrazza, the building was devastated. The roof had caved in. Flood waters invaded and left the floorboards buckled. Community members added insult to injury by looting and ransacking the facility. And for people with ties to the building, there was confusion and chaos. Unaware of the extent of the damage, staff members wondered if they should report to work. Brides were starting to ask if the venue would still be hosting their wedding. Cell phone service, meanwhile, was practically non-existent. There was nobody to go to, nobody to call. But you could drive by Titus' property on 34th Street and see the construction sign and emergency number. So, when phones started to work again, people started to call me. And very quickly, I was typecast as one of the bad guys in this disaster.

The venue on 34th Street, meanwhile, did not experience the level of destruction that Bella Terrazza suffered. But it would have needed all hands on board at Titus to get it up to speed for any kind of event. It would have needed an operating budget, too. None of that was happening because when Ike blew in town, Evil Dan blew out. And with him was what I guessed to be more than half of a million dollars in brides' deposits. Everything was unraveling. Evil Dan's mother and one-third partner, Carolyn James, speaking on behalf of Titus Inc., announced that both venues were closed permanently.

I learned later that the deposits Evil Dan had been collecting from brides and grooms, for both of his venues, were likely spent covering payments for other financial obligations, possibly from IRS payments to personal expenses. I also found out that Dan had been sending employees across the country to buy vintage video games, which he then stored in rented storage warehouses in different parts of the country. In my opinion he was not minding his existing business. The deposits he collected for events certainly weren't going for the construction of the facility. In reality, those deposits should have been set aside for the intended use of delivering those events. The only ones that know for sure are Evil Dan and his complicit mother, Carolyn, his bookkeeper. I remember Evil Dan saying that she was a CPA in her presence, and she would sit silently instead of objecting, though she most definitely was NOT a CPA. I believe there may have been more than one occasion when I witnessed her referring to herself as a CPA, as well.

Evil Dan's departure led three of The Brides of Harris

County (please see the book's introduction) to team up and force Titus Inc. into involuntary bankruptcy. My guess is they were hoping to at least get a portion of the money Titus had collected from them. The result was unsuccessful.

Shortly after that time, I realized personal bankruptcy was my only option. It was a logical conclusion, but the truth is, I was devastated. At that point, I felt my life was completely out of control.

To this day, I find it painful to think about that period.

I was at one of my lowest points ever. And people who were wronged by Titus started seeking me out.

It's safe to say that just like the Houston-Galveston area, my life was in bad shape by the time Ike moved on.

It would be years before I was able to see the events of that season with clarity. I remember papering my walls with letters, journal entries, and documents from that time, like a forensic investigator, trying to make sense of what happened.

I still don't have all of the answers. But I do believe that perhaps, even though I never would have asked for it, that storm propelled me to a better place, to the considerably better life that my family and I are experiencing today.

But getting to that place, that was quite the wild ride.

FINAL THOUGHTS ABOUT BOB

I LIVED WITH BOB FOR 20 YEARS AND KNEW him for more than 40 years. He was the best man at my wedding. I'd considered him my best friend. I'd trusted him with everything I had.

In the end, I felt I was deceived, and he didn't even seem aware of his actions' impact on my life. Only after it became clear I'd depleted all of my funds, my credit, and my company's goodwill, did Bob take notice. His response? He drove me to a bankruptcy attorney. There was no offer to help me financially. His assets were supposed to be securing the construction loans from his bank. But he didn't see any reason to sell his assets to cover his obligations to me.

My feelings about Bob have been very complicated since my dealings with Titus, but I never stopped loving him. And because I loved him, I provided Bob's memorial service after his death. I'm not sure whether we would have been able to heal our relationship if we'd been given more time. In the end, though, all I could control was the way I treated him. I'm glad I was able to give him a loving goodbye.

Bell Tower Trivia

THE BUILDING FOUNDATION OF THE
BELL TOWER ON 34TH WAS CURED
WITH REAL CHAMPAGNE.

Chapter 5

ACCEPTING A
NEW FUTURE

"WHEN JOHNNY CARRABBA GETS HERE, could you please ask him to pretend he knows me?"

Why would I ask one of Houston's best known and most successful restaurateurs to carry on a ruse that we were acquainted? It all boiled down to this: a shot at financial recovery.

Johnny, the man I was asking this humongous favor of, is the chef who co-founded the popular restaurant chain, Carrabba's Italian Grill. He and his uncle, Damian Mandola, opened the restaurant's first location in Houston more than 30 years ago. Today, the restaurant has more than 240 locations throughout the country. Johnny and Damian, while remaining active with their restaurant chain, also went on to host their own PBS cooking show, *Cucina Amore*, and write its companion cookbooks.

Johnny had already achieved this great success and acclaim in 2009, the year I asked the manager of the original Carrabba's location on Kirby Drive if Johnny wouldn't mind pretending that we knew each other. The odds of him helping me, or even taking my strange message seriously, were slim at best.

But when you're desperate, you surprise yourself with the things you're willing to do. My future was on the line that night. I was about to eat dinner with a potential investor with the money and power to rescue my family and me from the dire financial situation we found ourselves in. He and his father were actually considering investing in the nearly complete event venue on West 34th Street. And for some reason, they were under the impression that I knew Johnny well enough to recruit him to be the new venue's chef. (All right, I might have said something to that effect a few months earlier in an ill-advised effort to impress them.) I never imagined that when the potential investor and his wife visited Houston from their out-of-state home, that they'd want to meet my wife, Angela, and me for dinner. At Carrabba's. Where they could meet Johnny.

So, yes, I was willing to go pretty far to keep our budding business relationship with this potential investor viable.

But desperation wasn't my only motivator. For the first time in I don't know how long, I was hopeful. I found myself visualizing a better future for my family.

And I was determined to fight for that future.

THE CHUY INTERVENTION

I can't tell you how wonderful it felt around that time to find myself waking up without a feeling of dread.

Just a few months earlier, life was looking pretty hopeless. I didn't see any way out of the financial pit I found myself in, and the thing that really ate away at me was the fact that Angela and my kids were down there with me.

To be honest, I believe at any time we could have gotten financial support from Angela's parents. At one point, they offered to help me start a new business venture. And I did a few small projects with their help. I suspect that they provided more money behind the scenes to help us get by a few times, too, but I wasn't told about it. I'm sorry if you disagree, but to me there is something fundamental about a man's need to take care of his family without having to take handouts or get a big loan. Especially from his in-laws. I just didn't like that idea at all. It's not that I didn't appreciate my in-laws' desire to help us. But all in all, we were just in way too deep, and accepting my in-laws' financial help for too long would just have made things worse. I didn't want to go even deeper into debt. It was all getting to me. On more than one night, I found myself pacing up

Musicians: (left to right) me, Ricky Ford, and Chuy.

and down the driveway of our house, despondent and coming up empty on solutions.

Thankfully, it was around that time when God brought a man named Jesus "Chuy" Terrazas III back into my life, and with him, the encouragement that would propel me toward a better future.

Chuy had no ties with Titus Inc. or the Bella Terrazza venue, despite the similarity in names. I'd first met Chuy back in my days as a musician. Like me, Chuy played saxophone with a popular local group. We ran into each other at Houston-area venues, and over time, became friendly acquaintances.

Our paths remained strangely similar: We'd both

been in the music business and were also working in real estate, although at different ends of the spectrum. While I was the superintendent for a custom home builder, Chuy was buying little houses, fixing them up and leasing them out.

From time to time, we'd see each other at places like Home Depot and talk about our work and our goals. I still remember Chuy telling me something like, "I just rented my first house, and I'm hoping one day I'll have three or four."

By the next time we met, a few years later, I think he said he now owned 30 rental houses.

We continued to touch base here and there over the years. After I began the process of filing for bankruptcy, his name was on a list I made of people who might have connections that would help me dig my way back. My thought was, the path to making things better for my family had to start with someone purchasing the now abandoned wedding venue on 34th Street. Maybe someone could point me toward a potential buyer. I didn't know very much about how bankruptcies worked yet, but I reasoned that if someone purchased the venue, maybe pennies on the dollar from the sale would be used to pay me a bit of the money Titus Inc. still owed me.

I wasn't sure how, or if, everything would come together. I just knew how badly I wanted to give my unpaid subcontractors some of the money owed them. I'd be happy, for starters, to have enough money to pay for my children's back-to-school school clothes. Or buy a tank of gas.

Anyway, I figured Chuy had some local connections. So, I called him.

While Chuy didn't know anyone interested in buying a wedding venue, his decision to step up and be a friend during my lowest moments proved to be infinitely more valuable.

Chuy has a magical touch. He subscribes to the philosophy that thoughts manifest themselves: that what you think is what you become. I believe he felt that as my friend, it was his job to help me see the bright future that I couldn't yet envision for myself, to help me regain some of the optimism and determination he'd seen me demonstrate in the past.

Chuy always took my calls. He listened. He offered advice. *And he told me that he believed in me.*

"You know what to do, Roger," Chuy told me. "This is going to work out. This is going to be amazing for you."

Receiving that kind of support meant the world to me. Everyone else seemed to be saying the total opposite.

And Chuy wasn't merely being kind. He was very clear-minded and logical as he explained that a solution was indeed possible. Chuy insisted that somewhere in my mind I already knew what my next move was. When I stopped panicking, he said, it would come to me.

And he was right.

LIFELINES AND ANSWERED PRAYERS

Over the course of the days, weeks, and months following Hurricane Ike and during my bankruptcy, my mom sent small amounts of money for groceries on Kroger gift cards along with notes of encouragement. Those acts of love and support helped tremendously.

I know Mom and her prayer group must have prayed a thousand prayers during that period. So did I. When I was in the throes of deep desperation and didn't know at all where to turn or what to do, I got on my knees and I prayed to God even more. My career and my business had been ruined. I asked God for strength and courage. I prayed often.

One day, the solution came to me all at once.

I remember the first time I actually heard the words come out of my mouth. It was when I floated the idea to my mom. Not only would I find an investor who would buy the venue on 34th Street and let me complete the construction, but I would also become the tenant, run the business, and eventually, become the owner. My mom did not interrupt once while I described my new vision. She just listened and then gave pause. I remember waiting for her to offer other ideas or solutions, or maybe even disapproval or doubt. I waited for her to be the next one in the conversation to speak. She did not say anything for what seemed like an inordinate amount of time until, finally, as if to give permission, she said in an upbeat and firm voice, "OK." To me *it was during that remarkable silence that the God-given vision for the journey I was about to embark on was validated. And then it was verbally approved.*

It was all so clear, and now I knew what I had to do. *There were no other alternatives.*

Before long I had a similar conversation with Angela. "Wouldn't it be amazing if…," I started. This would be for our family. This would be a way to try and make things OK. It was a long shot. We would try to make the place what it was always meant to be from the start. Maybe even better.

Without any sign of doubt or skepticism, she nodded, smiled, and agreed. I can tell you Angela has a beautiful smile. *But the smile she had on her face during that conversation on that day, and the look in her eyes, are what gave me the inspiration to go for it.* It was like she was giving me the green light to try and make the impossible happen. Approved!

I don't know what I would have done without the encouragement and prayers of my mom and the unwavering love and support I received from Angela.

Once I had a solution, and my family's support, I was able to map out a plan for making it happen. First of all, I needed someone to buy the venue property as an investment. As I approached potential buyers, I offered to make them a return of $1 million. (This was a risky move. I'd been taught NEVER to suggest that any kind of financial return on an investment was possible. Thank goodness doing so did not backfire.)

The buyers, in return, would need to agree to certain requirements.

- I would be their real estate representative when they bought the property.

- After that, I would be the contractor who completed the building's construction (it just needed a few finishing touches at that point).

- At the same time, I would be the investor's tenant: I would be the president and CEO of the wedding venue, responsible for opening it and building a thriving business.

- And finally, I would have the irrevocable right to buy the building from the investor at any time during the term of our lease.

After approaching dozens of people, I connected with a very special man. He and his father, who owned a capital investment firm, agreed to listen to my proposal.

Of course, they had a few stipulations of their own.

THE CHEF DILEMMA

My prospective investors, known to their friends and family as Shrub and Branch, said that if they were to invest in our venue, they would want a well-established and well-known chef to make the deal more palatable for investment.

I told them we already were considering several candidates for that role.

But the investors already had someone in mind. You guessed it: celebrity chef Johnny Carrabba. If I could get him, my investment proposition would look like a real winner in Shrub and Branch's eyes.

But could I get him?

Well, I had met Johnny. Sort of. A couple of years previously I had attended a charity event where Johnny had volunteered to donate his services as an auction item. He offered to prepare and serve a dinner for 12 at the winning bidder's home. A friend of Angela's won the bid, and she and I were among her friend's dinner guests when Johnny came over to cook.

That was the extent of my dealings with Johnny up to then.

But because I REALLY wanted Shrub and Branch to move forward with a deal, I found myself telling them that I knew Johnny. In fact, I told them recruiting him to be my chef was a real possibility.

My backup plan could be to recruit an equally awesome alternative to be our venue's chef after the investment deal was finalized, and everyone would be happy.

Actually, you could say I had a few backup plans in the works. At the same time we were having discussions about Johnny, I was also bringing up the name of another very famous Houston chef named Bruce Molzan, who studied under Wolfgang Puck. I knew Bruce from his days at Ruggles Grill, when he personally hired and helped promote my band, Global Village. Before The Bell Tower on 34th opened, I had conversations with Bruce and his business partner, Robert Guillerman, about joining our company's board of advisors. I'm glad that did not pan out: Years later Bruce received some very bad press. My point is, Johnny's name came up as more of a Plan B. Ironically, our first chef, Chef Gilbert, was a former sous chef under Bruce. Small world. As Paul Harvey would say, that's the "rest of the story."

Anyhow, very soon after our conversation about Johnny, I got a call from Branch. He and his wife were planning a visit to Houston from out of state and wanted to go out to dinner with Angela and me. "Let's meet over at Carrabba's, and we'll even get to meet this chef of yours," Branch said.

All I could think was, I'm in BIG trouble.

At that point I was still broke, so broke that I'd resorted to digging beneath couch cushions and rummaging through every drawer in the house in search of change. As I remember it, that's how I came up with the gas money I needed to drive Angela to our dinner date with Branch and his wife.

Forget scrimping together enough money for our meal. I tried and failed. And of course, as someone who was in the middle of filing for bankruptcy, I couldn't use credit cards to pay. So here I was: I was supposed to be schmoozing an investor, but had no idea how I was going to pay for dinner. And, oh yeah, the celebrity chef my guests wanted to meet had no idea who I was.

At the time, Angela didn't know that we didn't have the money to cover our restaurant check. She certainly didn't know I'd "hinted" that I knew Johnny to the potential investor. When the night of our dinner date arrived, we dressed up and got ourselves to the Carrabba's Grill on Kirby drive. I knew that out of all the Carrabba's locations, this was where Johnny was reporting to work.

The moment we arrived, I asked for the manager and made my desperate request: If Johnny could stop by our table and say "hi," it would really mean a lot to me. Today, I realize this request was more than an act of desperation: It was one of the first—and most dramatic—steps I took to fight for a better future. This was Roger, refusing to give up.

Of course, I had no idea if my gamble would work. At the table with Angela, Branch, and his wife, I was really sweating it. Eating and making pleasant conversation required Herculean efforts. Focusing was a struggle.

That's when Johnny Carrabba stepped up to our table with a big smile on his face, his arms opened wide as if to offer a hug.

"Roger, how are you?" he asked, acting like we were old friends. "I haven't seen you in a long time!" I introduced him to my prospective investor and his wife. They shook hands. "Tonight, dinner is on me."

I can only imagine the look of utter relief that must have been on my face.

Even better, from what I remember Branch and his wife insisted on leaving the tip. We parted on a positive note. I think that must have been the night our prospective investors decided to do the deal because within weeks, Shrub and Branch began finalizing the details of our investment agreement.

I don't know if I can ever express to Johnny how grateful I am for his incredibly gracious actions that evening. I still wonder, sometimes, why he decided to help me or if he even has any idea of the impact on our lives he made that night. I hope, one day, to share the full story with him and thank him in person. Not only did Johnny help me preserve the much-needed favor I'd started to earn from Shrub and Branch, he also gave me the confidence to keep on fighting for my dream. And no, I never did line up Johnny to be our chef. But we did find a great culinary talent to fill that spot.

Today, I try to host a meeting over dinner with our senior staff at Carrabba's periodically, and all of our new hires hear the "Carrabba's Story." On your journey, I tell them (as Chuy used to say to me), don't wait for all of the traffic lights along the way to turn green before you move forward toward your goals. And remember, *anything* is possible. Don't give up. Keep on going. In the weeks ahead, I'd need to cling to that philosophy tightly.

Bell Tower Trivia

MORE THAN 80,000 CINDER BLOCKS
WERE BUILT INTO OUR BUILDING'S
BELL TOWER, EACH OF THEM PLACED
BY HAND.

Chapter 6

FINAL HURDLES

S HRUB AND BRANCH WEREN'T THE ONLY potential investors I was in communication with, though I must admit, I felt a real connection with them. They were empathetic to my situation and were well respected as businessmen. Nevertheless, two additional parties showed interest in my proposal, and I wasn't about to turn them away. I had no way of knowing how many other possible interested buyers were out there. But I assumed there must have been at least several others due to the amount of publicity the property had gotten in the news months earlier.

No matter who bought the wedding venue, it wouldn't be a simple real estate transaction. In addition to my requirements, there was the Titus Inc. factor. Because Titus had declared bankruptcy, the judge overseeing their case would also have to approve any purchase, even if the buyers were the investors I lined up.

When informed about the possibility of an investor buying the venue, the judge stated that all interested parties would have to come to court with a sealed bid. The purchase would be cash only with a set minimum.

Once the judge made that stipulation, two of my three potential investor groups decided to opt out. That left Shrub and Branch, and they ended up bidding below the minimum. I still remember the tidal wave of anxiety that washed over me when I learned they wouldn't be bidding the minimum amount. I was sick to my stomach. The property and its situation had been a topic of great public interest. I was sure other people would jump at the opportunity to bid. When I presented Shrub and Branch's sealed bid, I wanted to see who the other bidders were. Maybe I'd see a familiar name or face. But no one else presented the judge an offer: It was just me with an envelope.

Strangely, after my initial panicked reaction, I had a sensation of calmness or stillness about me. There was something about the demeanor of Shrub and all his financial wisdom that put me at ease. I felt as if maybe he had more information but wasn't telling anyone. I felt and trusted his wisdom.

In the end, the judge approved the bid from Shrub and Branch. I was elated. This was exactly what I needed to continue pushing toward my new goals.

But not all the news was good: Though the bankruptcy judge gave me permission to act as the buyers' broker, I wouldn't be entitled to any real estate commission, something I was counting on.

Typically, a seller's agent and a buyer's agent split the commission, about 2 or 3 percent of the purchase price, from a real estate transaction. In this instance, the trustees of the bankruptcy had hired the seller's real estate agent. At the last minute, the trustees appealed to the bankruptcy judge that since I did not present a buyer representation agreement, which the sellers easily could have requested from me, they would not offer to share or split any commission of the sale. I would have been OK with that, but instead of leaving the buyer's representative portion of the commission out of the transaction, they kept both sides of the real estate commission for themselves.

In one fell swoop, the bankruptcy trustees and judge had swung a wrecking ball at the first pillar of my financial recovery plan and turned it to rubble. Yes, you could say my thoughts were a bit dark after that turn of events.

TIME FOR CLOSURE

I did, however, have an ace up my sleeve. Months earlier, when the arrival of Hurricane Ike was imminent, I realized that I seriously needed to take additional steps to protect my financial interests. I went as far as drawing up and signing a contract to buy the property on 34th Street in its unfinished condition for $6.5 million—a deal that was signed off on by Evil Dan's mother, Carolyn, one of the Titus principals. I believed she signed it just as she was realizing Titus would never be able to pay me what was owed.

Eventually, I accepted the fact that I was in no financial position to buy anything. So, the contract was left sitting with Stewart Title Company.

However, while I was in the process of executing that contract, I also made a point of signing an *affidavit of contract* and filing it with the county clerk's office. This is not standard procedure for buyers; it's more of an extra safeguard. Because of that affidavit, my signature would be needed before anyone else could purchase the property, even if the property was being sold out of bankruptcy. Maybe, I thought, I'd be able to exchange my signature for cash at some point. I didn't have a real plan fleshed out when I filed the affidavit. I was just trying to use my knowledge as a licensed real estate broker, and every measure I could think of, to protect myself and my family from further financial losses. I didn't give it much more thought until I learned I'd be ineligible to receive a buyer's agent commission on the venue sale.

As for the pennies on the dollar I'd once hoped to collect from the sale of Titus' abandoned wedding venue, I wouldn't be seeing them. Even though I'm the one who brought all of the buyers to the table, the bankruptcy trustees were going to split the proceeds from the sale between the bank that had handled Titus' construction loan and the bankruptcy trustees' law firm. The money would be used to cover some of the bank's outstanding payments, interest, and the lawyers. This was the same bank that had waived Titus' performance bond requirement—a requirement that would have protected my business and subcontractors from Titus' inability to pay us—before approving Titus' loan in the first place.

All of these things were weighing on my mind as we approached the day of Shrub and Branch's closing on the property on 34th Street. Because of the affidavit of a contract I'd filed with the county clerk, my signature would be required before the purchase could be finalized. I did briefly fantasize about demanding a check from the seller's broker before I signed anything, but of course, I still very much wanted my investors' purchase to succeed. To me, scrapping the sale was never an option. But using the affidavit to mess with the minds of some of the people who'd messed with my business, my family, and me was an attractive possibility.

It was so attractive, in fact, that I approached Shrub and Branch and sought their permission to use the affidavit of a contract to get a bit of revenge. They knew much of what I'd gone through during the last year and that I was stressed. "Everything is going to be fine," I promised. "Please let me do this for me."

And this is how cool they were: they said, "Yep, do it." I'm sure it was because of our mutual trust.

And so, the morning of the closing arrived. Shrub and Branch signed their paperwork, and the title company wired their payment to the bankruptcy trustees. About an hour later, the trustees added their signatures.

That left me sitting at the closing table with a piece of paper, a pen, and the title company people standing around me, waiting for me to legally state in writing that I was terminating my earlier real estate contract to purchase the venue property and authorizing someone else to buy it.

And, of course, I was going to sign it. But aside from Shrub and Branch, no one knew that.

I could see the bankruptcy trustees, their lawyers, and the representatives from the bank waiting in the lobby. I said, "You know what, I'm not going to sign this." I briefly summarized how I'd been wronged by one person after another, from top to bottom. "I'm here, but I've had a change of heart," I said, rising from the table.

And I left.

At that point, one document was separating the bankruptcy trustees and bank from their millions. One document and one person: me.

My emotions remained intense through most of that day. I wanted to give some of the people who'd wronged me a taste of the heaping servings of stress that they'd dished out to me. *And I did.* After I refused to sign, the trustee's real estate agent drove to the venue property, changed the locks, and chained up the building. It would be accurate to say they were a bit agitated. I wanted to call them and ask them how it felt to get a bit of the treatment they'd given me!

Just before the close of business, only minutes before 5 p.m., I returned to the room where the closing had been taking place. It was full of people in suits and ties—mostly title company higher ups and attorneys—and I could hear them discussing their dilemma and options. When they saw me standing in the doorway, they all froze in silence.

I walked in, sat down, and said, "I'm going to sign."

I had never felt more respected. Everyone in the room was so relieved to see me. It felt like they were giving me a standing ovation. *For the first time in a long time, it felt like I was in charge.*

Not only that, Shrub and Branch ended up generously writing me a check for tens of thousands of dollars anyway, around the amount I would have received as a broker's commission, after the closing. Just like my gratitude for Johnny Carrabba, it's difficult to express how much their act of kindness meant to me.

The property closing, and the days leading up to it, could be described as one of the most emotionally intense chapters of my ordeal with Titus Inc. As I write about it, I can see a picture of a man who'd been deceived, manipulated, and pushed around until he was forced to make a decision. I could have given up, or I could claw and scratch my way to a better reality. I chose the latter. Signing the affidavit of a contract was an early step. Finding and securing investors was another, even more significant one. But giving some of the people who'd done me wrong a taste of their own medicine, that was a major turning point. That small gesture of revenge went a long way toward making things feel right—or at least on their way to right. From that point on, I continued fighting for a better future for my family and myself.

Of course, that wasn't really on my mind after the closing. All I knew then was I'd gone from a bankrupt general contractor to the man who'd soon be opening and operating Houston's newest wedding and special events venue.

It had been a tense moment, and the emotional roller-coaster ride I'd started when I started seeking investors to buy the venue was far from over.

Bell Tower Trivia

CHEF SERGIO ARELLANO HAS OVERSEEN
THE PREPARATION OF MORE THAN 6
MILLION MEALS IN HIS CAREER.

Chapter 7

WITHIN OUR GRASP

ONE OF THE MOST CRITICAL FIGURES IN my journey up to that point—aside from God, my wife, and mother—was my friend Chuy. There's no doubt that he was a lifeline during some of my darkest hours during and after my bankruptcy.

Looking back, I wish I had simply embraced Chuy's encouragement and guidance and stopped there. Instead, as he, Angela, and I discussed plans for working with an investor and establishing a wedding venue on 34th Street, we began to draw Chuy into those plans. By the time we worked out the details, Chuy, Angela, and I committed to be partners along with a fourth woman I'll call Jessica, who was a friend of Chuy's. I respected Chuy for his success and had seen firsthand how he cultivated an empire of small rental properties (and eventually huge apartment complexes). So, I saw his partnership as a tremendous opportunity. And I also trusted his judgment when he said that Jessica's knowledge of the food and beverage industry would help us market our venue, not only to couples planning weddings, but also to businesses, organizations, and families.

I have to say, looking back, Chuy's input was valuable, yet tremendously frustrating at times, during the process of legally establishing our business and negotiating a lease with our investors. He didn't pressure us to work with Jessica: We agreed to the partnership after meeting with her several times. She clearly knew a lot about the food and beverage business. I had every reason to be optimistic about our future together as business partners.

The first cracks in my business relationship with Chuy appeared shortly after we discussed our financial commitments to the business. You may remember that when Shrub and Branch agreed to invest in the wedding venue, they had a few stipulations. One was securing a well-known chef. Another requirement was a commitment on our part: We would have at least $350,000 in our business' bank account within six months of signing our lease.

This was a reasonable request. Our investors knew that we'd need significant cash reserves to protect our new company during the inevitable ups and downs we'd be facing. If a customer or two failed to pay us on time, or we encountered a lag in business, we'd still be able to cover our expenses.

Angela, Chuy, Jessica, and I were confident we'd be

able to generate the $350,000. For starters, we would each put $5,000 of our own funds into the bank. That would be more than a step toward the total: We needed it for a long list of start-up costs, from filing our new business' paperwork with the state to paying an attorney to help draw up our lease.

As for the full $350,000, we all agreed it would be tough, but we felt we could raise the capital, possibly by asking friends and acquaintances for support.

The day arrived for the four partners to meet at our bank, open an account for our business, and deposit our contributions.

Up to that day, Chuy had been saying that instead of the $20,000 we planned to deposit, he was confident we'd be able to put as much as $50,000 in the bank. He figured I'd be contributing Angela's share as well as mine, and with my contractor's pay, I'd be able to surpass my agreed upon amount.

He was right, to some degree. Angela and I arrived at the bank with $25,000. Basically, it was my "getting-started money" as a contractor fee for Shrub and Branch, and some of the real estate "commission" money they'd given me.

Jessica was a no-show that day, but she asked Chuy to contribute her portion of the deposit, and she'd reimburse him.

Chuy, meanwhile, told us at the last minute that he wasn't going to put in his agreed-upon contribution. *He was only going to supply a percentage of that.*

We were shocked. Our partnership was predicated

on the idea that we'd all be putting in equal amounts of money.

We were able to open our business' bank account, but everything felt different from that point on.

Not only that, but Jessica quickly became more of a liability than an asset. When we planned partners' meetings, she'd show up, stay for a few minutes and leave, claiming she had somewhere else to be.

We'd ask her about contributing money. She'd change the subject. At one point, Jessica did write us a check for a small amount, a check that bounced. She apologized, saying she'd accidentally used a check from an account she'd closed, and gave us a check drawn upon a different account. That check failed to clear, too.

Our four-way partnership would continue to struggle after we opened our doors for business.

LA PROMESA

During the venue's initial construction, I "completed" the building for Evil Dan and delivered the project under what was called a "temporary certificate of occupancy." However, there was still a great deal to be done before the place would be totally completed. When I returned to the construction process, we continued with the venue's original architectural plans. However, I knew one thing had to change: our new business' name. The Tuscany of Garden Oaks was too closely associated with Titus Inc. and Evil Dan.

Our working name during round two of construction

was La Promesa, which is both Spanish and Italian for "the promise." The name seemed fitting: I was fulfilling the promise made to our investors by completing construction and preparing to open the venue for business. It was a fulfillment of what the place was always meant to be.

But I didn't feel a Spanish name was the right long-term choice. The venue's Old World design is intentionally ambiguous: It draws a bit from Spanish architecture—and also from Italian building styles. The partners agreed; we wanted to leave some interpretation open to the eyes of each client.

Not only that, we also wanted to host corporate events in addition to weddings. We just couldn't picture a couple of execs on the golf course saying, "We're going to have our next corporate event at La Promesa." I don't know; it sounded too "weddingy" to us.

I started thinking, if someone had seen our building and was mentioning it to someone else, how would they refer to it? They'd probably call it something like, "that bell tower on 34th Street." That was it! We all agreed and named our new venue The Bell Tower on 34th. It's direct, simple, and calls the building what it is.

The next challenge was creating an environment that, just like the venue's name, would resonate equally well with both corporate and wedding clients. With Branch's blessings, we consulted with one of the best interior designers we knew: Angela's mom.

Glenda Nicholson spent hours helping us choose paint colors and navigate other challenging design decisions. The main color of our building is her selection. She helped us acquire fantastic French chandeliers dating back more than 100 years (please see page 154) for the Contessa Ballroom. She also helped us purchase armoires and other antiques—and even provided pieces from her own collection. Glenda's contributions truly helped The Bell Tower on 34th shine, and we have her to thank for the many compliments our venue receives for its charm and beauty.

The experience of building a new business, including the literal building process, was exhilarating. The venue was coming together, and it was stunning. Complementing Glenda's expert design touches were the stones, heavy doors, and chandeliers that Evil Dan and I found during our trip to Mexico. I started working in a few additional special touches as well.

One of my favorites was the "Old Chicago" brick that we incorporated into several of our rooms. The brick was apparently reclaimed from structures lost to the Great Chicago Fire, which burned for three days in October 1871. The fire had been tragic: Several hundred people lost their lives in it; 100,000 others lost their homes; and 3.3 square miles of Chicago were destroyed in the blaze. To me, the bricks that remained were symbols of survival, a picture of a building anew out of the ashes.

Plus, the bricks are gorgeous. Chicago brick was made mostly with grayish blue clay from the region, which turned salmon or buff colors after being fired in an oven. Their presence adds something special to the overall atmosphere of the rooms.

A NEW HIRE AND VISITORS

Before I even began completing the venue's construction, I realized that as the general contractor, I'd need someone to help me with bookkeeping. I knew some of the people who'd worked for Titus Inc. before its bankruptcy, good people who were now unemployed, and offered one of them, Sarah, part-time work managing my books. She became our first real employee. Sarah started working from our house, where Angela and I had transformed a large closet into a command center of sorts. Sarah had a set of filing cabinets, our home computer, and one phone line that doubled as a fax line. Some days, I brought Sarah to the construction office we'd set up at the venue. There, her desk was a small folding table.

Several empty shops still sat on the site where The Bell Tower on 34th was being built. The one I was using as my construction office had been a lawn mower shop for years. Apparently, word about the shop's closure had been slow to circulate in the community, because several people stopped by while I was there, hoping to drop off their lawn equipment for repairs. One very nearsighted elderly gentleman was especially insistent and didn't seem to believe me when I told him I couldn't fix his lawnmower for him.

We had other visitors, too. Some wanted to tell their stories from the Bill Mraz Dance Hall days.

"Do you have any idea what this place used to be?" they'd ask. The dance hall was the backdrop to some of their favorite memories. Some had met their spouses there. It was difficult for them to imagine a different business at that address.

And, of course, angry Titus Inc. creditors noticed the construction as well. Some went to online wedding planning sites and blogs to warn people that the evil business they'd fallen victim to was preparing to prey upon more unsuspecting people.

I established a protocol for these visits. If anyone visiting our building or offices so much as hinted about the venue's past or the bankruptcy situation in any way, workers would politely interrupt them and summon me. I would drop everything I was doing, talk with that person, and provide the full story. That was the only approach I could think of to minimize the spread of misinformation about the new venue. Unfortunately, my open-door policy dramatically cut into my productivity. Sometimes those conversations took a few hours. People got emotional. They vented. And I needed them to listen to my side of the story. After a while, I started keeping an organized packet of information in my briefcase, sort of like visuals for a business presentation, so I could better explain what had happened with Titus and clear my name.

Even meeting with prospective customers was complicated. What I usually heard from them was, "I see this is a beautiful place you're going to be opening, but my mom and dad are very skeptical because they heard that you were involved with the previous project. What guarantee do we have that you won't run off with our money?" So, there were more long conversations and presentations of the facts.

Our soon-to-open venue attracted the interest of other people, too. We started getting phone calls from people who wanted our business and support, from linen suppliers to photographers and limo services hoping we'd recommend them to our eventual customers.

It was an intense period. I was very close to surviving one of the most traumatic periods of my life. I was living a miracle and continuing to push forward toward my goal, but I was exhausted. Every day was a stream of prospective client meetings, the work of getting the venue completed and ready for business, and reporting back to our investors, all while taking impromptu meetings with angry Titus Inc. creditors. I had no real office, minimal staff, and was just trying to get to where we could finish the place and hopefully open.

But I did take time to do something extra, something to create a little symbol of optimism for my family and me, something that would encourage us as we pushed toward the finish line.

TIME CAPSULE

On the marble floor of one of our venue ballrooms was an ornate medallion, a compass rose star that was destroyed by vandals while the building was sitting vacant. Looking at it, I started envisioning that spot as something more than a decorative feature. I imagined it as the "X" that marked the spot, so to speak, for a buried treasure. Except in our case, that treasure could be a time capsule. So, after picking up the pieces of the original marble medallion from the floor, we had a worker remove a cylindrical core from the building's concrete foundation. The process was pretty interesting. The worker used a drill bit the size of a tree trunk, about 12 to 15 inches in diameter, to remove the concrete. He then excavated the dirt below to make room for our tube-shaped time capsule, which was made of PVC pipe. We filled our capsule with everything we could think of at the moment: newspaper clippings about the Bill Mraz Dance Hall, a couple of my business cards, preliminary information about our venue, 2009 currency. I can't even remember everything we placed

Our children were happy to place our time capsule beneath the floor of our main ballroom.

in there, but I do remember that on the day of our time capsule installation, Angela and I and our children held a short ceremony and took pictures of our kids placing the capsule into the hole in the floor. We sealed up the hole and topped it with a new marble medallion.

Today, when people enter our venue's foyer, they're greeted with a small bronze sign that says, "A time capsule is located directly beneath the compass rose star at the center of the main ballroom. The capsule was placed by the family of the venue's original builder on Aug. 29, 2009."

Today, the time capsule is a nice marketing tool. But when I placed it, it gave me a way to make my mark, so to speak. Getting to that point had been such an incredible, emotional journey. And there were so many moments when it was not at all certain that everything would come together. In fact, even as we installed the time capsule, I still didn't know for sure that I'd be able to open the venue and make it a success. Sure, I had ambitions; I had some big goals, and I was determined to make them realities. But in some ways, my efforts to transform myself from a bankrupt general contractor to an event venue CEO and owner was kind of a Hail Mary. Secretly, deep down, I wasn't sure if it was going to work.

So, this time capsule was my way of stamping my name on this building. Maybe when I'm dead and gone someone will come and find the time capsule. They'll open it up, and my name will come out. And I'll be forever linked with the venue's history.

Bell Tower Trivia

WE ONCE HAD A BRIDE, WHO AFTER
BREAKING UP WITH HER FIANCÉ,
ASKED US TO KEEP HER DEPOSIT AND
HOLD HER DATE. SHE SAID SHE WOULD
FIND ANOTHER MAN WILLING TO
MARRY HER BY THEN—AND SHE DID!

Chapter 8

OPEN FOR BUSINESS

I N ONE OF THE BEST SCENES IN THE COMEDY movie *Mrs. Doubtfire*, Robin Williams' character, disguised as a female nanny, fails at his first attempt to make dinner on the job when he burns the Hollandaise sauce and catches his silicon body suit on fire. Williams' character saves the day and protects Mrs. Doubtfire's image as a nanny extraordinaire by paying more than $100 for restaurant delivery and presenting the meal as if he cooked it.

Sixteen years after that classic comedy appeared in theaters, I found myself in a bit of the same jam. No padded body suits or fires were involved, but I did have to think fast when the chef that The Bell Tower on 34th had lined up for the evening cancelled at the last minute. It was our first event since we had opened our business.

Looking back, that chef probably was only halfway committed to us. He agreed to help us, but he may have wondered if we were actually going to be open for business by the time our first event rolled around. He ended up accepting a side catering job for someone else on the same evening, and he didn't tell us he'd opted out of our event until it was only a night or two away. I will never forget how he treated that situation. We were very disappointed.

And we were stressed.

Our shiny new customer, a title company, had booked our venue for a poker party. And during that process, we'd presented them with a menu based on our would-be chef's signature dishes. The customer's selections included a chicken and pasta dinner with the chef's amazing homemade marinara sauce. That meant we needed someone who could provide a close match.

Somehow, I found a drop-off caterer who could fill in at the last minute. They could even make chicken with pasta. But they didn't offer that kind of marinara sauce.

After a frantic search, I remembered another chef I knew, Tim Mehne, who agreed to make the fresh marinara sauce. Tim dropped off the marinara sauce separately from the catering company, barely in the nick of time. So, just like Mrs. Doubtfire, I found a way to meet my customer's expectations, even though it called for spending way too much money on takeout.

(Tim, by the way, had been in the food and beverage industry for more than 35 years when he helped me and had served as executive chef of the both the Astrodome in Houston and the Superdome in New Orleans. He has said that the best moments for him involved teaching and empowering employees and mentoring youth. My kind of chef!)

We must have done something right that evening, because the title company returned for another party the following year.

But it was clear that even though I completed the Herculean tasks of finding a buyer for the event venue, finishing construction, and opening for business, we weren't out of the woods just yet. We'd have to keep pushing, to continue fighting and scrambling, to make this business work.

STANDING OUR GROUND

By the time we held our first event, our leadership team had seen a significant change. Angela, Chuy, and I realized we had to address the lack of support our new business was receiving from our fourth partner, Jessica. She made promises of financial support that she never delivered. And even though we could have used the money, what we really counted on was her experience in the food and beverage business. But there, too, she failed us. As I mentioned, when we needed her input at our periodic partner meetings, she'd skate in and leave moments after arriving, claiming she had somewhere else to be. We didn't exactly feel like our company was important to her.

Jessica continued as a partner—at least on paper—until we completed the venue's construction and held an open house to introduce our new business to the community in September 2009.

One month or so after our open house, the partners, including Chuy, unanimously decided that Jessica simply hadn't fulfilled her partnership obligations. Our only recourse was to terminate our partnership with her.

By the time we made the decision to end the business relationship with her, it was a relief. Angela and I had a very difficult phone call with Jessica, to tell her our business relationship wasn't working out, and we finally said goodbye. It was both tense and emotional, but it was necessary: We had to keep the business moving forward.

RENTAL WELCOME MATS

When we opened The Bell Tower on 34th in fall 2009, the venue was everything I'd hoped it would be, with elegant ballrooms, sweeping staircases, and lush landscaping and gardens. But in many ways, we were doing without. Behind the scenes, we had no real offices, no carpet, no phone lines, no finished ceilings. Many parts of the building lacked light switches: When Evil Dan originally planned the building, he had decided lights would only be controlled by the breaker boxes, which was not a good decision. We also had minimal electrical outlets and no dimmers for adjusting the lighting.

Because our financial resources were on the low side by the time we finished construction, hiring more people, or even buying basics like plates and linens, were out of the question. Instead, we "rented" staff from an agency. And we rented serving equipment. And dishes. And nearly everything we needed to host events. We were even renting our welcome mats.

There were a few exceptions. Out of the blue, Chuy bought us a computer and put down money for our first liquor inventory. And Branch, one of our investors, even loaned us an additional $25,000 to help us purchase tables and chairs. Another generous act.

I was determined to get the business past this renting phase. I remember calculating our equipment rental costs per piece, comparing them to purchase costs, and figuring out how many events it would take before each purchase would pay for itself. A full set of buffet serving equipment, for example, might take one or two events to pay for itself when compared to renting the same gear. On the other hand, I'd have to serve 150,000 entrees before the top-of-the-line commercial oven I'd been eyeing would pay for itself. Armed with that information, I created a descending expense report on a per-event basis so we could prioritize purchases. Then, little by little, we transitioned from renting to owning the items we used.

I remember when we bought our welcome mats. They were among the first group of "expensive" things we purchased, and buying them, to me, was a milestone. It took three months of delivering events for them to pay for themselves. Odd as it may seem, when we bought them I thought, we are a viable business now. Our determination is paying off. We can make it.

Building up staff was a gradual process, too. Initially, my accounting manager Sarah was our only employee. Next, I hired two salespeople to work wedding expos, and we added more people, little by little, as we went along. It took a long time to ease our dependence on hospitality industry temporary staffing agencies. They're easy to use: You call and tell them you need 10 waiters. They send them. If your request exceeds a certain number, they send a seasoned waitstaff worker, a "captain," who will help ensure your large event runs smoothly. But, over time we were able to start bringing in and training our own waitstaff. Today, depending on the season, The Bell Tower on 34th might employ 80 to 100 great full and part-time people.

During those early days, every event we lined up, every deposit we made at the bank, was a thrill, another affirmation that our tenacity was netting results, and we were on our way. Despite the concerns we heard from some before we opened that we would be responsible for "The Brides of Harris County, The Sequel," plenty of people were willing to give us a chance. I think they were drawn to the beauty of our venue and its convenient Houston location. And, of course, we actively worked on bringing in business. Our initial focus was on weddings. In fact, one of the first things we did after we signed our lease was to organize ourselves for the July Bridal Extravaganza in Houston. And we advertised in four wedding magazines. For years, our marketing efforts comprised advertising in those magazines, the summer and winter bridal shows, and our website. And it worked. For the most part.

A BIT OF LUCK, FAITH, AND PRAYER

As part of our deal with Shrub and Branch, they allowed us to operate for six months before we started paying them rent. The idea was to give us time to get situated and line up customers. We also were supposed to have $350,000 in the bank after six months, as I mentioned earlier.

We had been optimistic about meeting the savings requirement. But as a new business, we were operating hand to mouth, even with our frugal approach to spending. We did put some money in the bank, but nothing close to the amount Shrub and Branch had in mind. Angela and I worried they would swoop in and take over the business, but as the deadline approached, they stopped asking about our savings—probably because we were so prompt with our rent payments.

Looking back over our history as tenants, we only struggled to make rent two times. The first time we ran short, I admit we attempted a bluff in the same vein as our dinner with Branch at Carrabba's, when I pretended I knew the restaurant chain's founder and chef. On the day our very first rent payment was due, I called Shrub and made an appointment to visit his out-of-town office later that next week. We were going to make a ceremony of presenting our first rent check. I remember telling Shrub that we wanted to give him the check in person and have our picture taken. At first, he disagreed with the idea and suggested wiring the money. We could stage a photo any time, he pointed out. I held my ground: It would be much more meaningful to use the real rent check, I insisted.

Of course, we were stalling. We didn't have enough money. But, somehow, we were able to gather the rest of it in time for our check presentation and photo shoot. I'm not absolutely sure, but I think we must still have that photo of us in Shrub's office. It was a little scary, but that was how we were getting by—by the skin of our teeth.

Our second late rent payment occurred during the summer of 2010. We could see it coming. We were running low on cash because business was still ramping up, and we were still relatively new, but we had been in talks with several potential customers about booking our venue for last-minute events. We'd been praying that someone would sign a contract, and we would deliver more events soon.

On the Friday our rent was due, Angela and I were driving our children out of town for summer camp, which their grandparents were paying for. That Saturday, Shrub called and left a message, surprised I hadn't wired the rent. I was west of San Antonio, in an area known as Texas Hill Country. In those days cell phone service was spotty in that area, and I was able to truthfully use that as an excuse for failing to call back.

I'd been hoping that, miraculously, we'd get our rent money together that day. We didn't. Finally, I got the courage up to call Shrub. I apologized for the poor cell service and prayerfully acted as though it was a given that Shrub would soon be receiving his money. Based on our lease, rent was due on the first of the month, and if we failed to pay within 10 days, we would be in default. I tried framing that 10-day period in a more positive light. "I thought we had a 10-day grace period to pay the rent," I told Shrub. Thankfully, he didn't press the subject, even though I could tell he wasn't happy. On the following Monday, we were able to pay our rent before it was too late. After that, business remained steady, then began growing. To be clear, I know my stalling tactics were not good business practices. I'm not proud of my actions, but we did what we had to do in those days to survive. Sometimes, you surprise yourself with what you're willing to do when the stakes are high. At least we didn't give up. And we were never late with rent again.

Years later when I applied for a mortgage to finally buy the venue property, Shrub wrote a letter on behalf of Angela and me, saying we "monotonously" paid our rent. We were able to purchase the property four years and one month after signing our lease. To this day, I'm grateful for him and that he chose to remember the many times we did pay on time, instead of those two times we didn't.

TIME OF TRANSITION

My friend Chuy was a source of hope during one of the darkest periods of my life, when my personal finances were in ruin, and I was starting to give up on myself. His unwavering encouragement got me through the despair and helped me see my way out of the mental, emotional, and financial pit I was in.

And as a partner, Chuy did make contributions to The Bell Tower on 34th. For example, he offered helpful advice while we were finalizing our lease agreement with our investors, Shrub and Branch. And it was Chuy who bought the business its first computer. He paid for our initial liquor inventory, too. (Though later, against my better judgment, I let him reclaim some of the beverage inventory for himself. At that point, I was still hopeful that Chuy's business acumen would help us keep moving forward toward our goals.)

That's why thinking about Chuy today brings tremendously mixed emotions. Though Chuy was a true friend when I needed one most, and he did help our business get on its feet, his contributions are overshadowed by the times he let me down and, at times, even moved our goals further from our reach.

Take the personal referrals he made. He sent any number of friends and clients to book events at The Bell Tower on 34th. And while this sounded good on the surface, the problem was, every single one of them made it clear that as a friend of Chuy's, they expected deep discounts. I'm talking huge, ridiculously below cost discounts. Even though I think at the time he had good intentions, it truly seemed like instead of fostering stability, Chuy was moving our fledgling business in the wrong direction.

Basically, Angela and I felt that vastly disproportionate amounts of capital were put into our business—Angela and I *each* contributed something like 225 percent more than Chuy did—all while the three of us owned equal shares of the company. That did not even account for the amount of time spent working on the business itself to make it great. It felt like Chuy was getting a free ride and benefitting from our efforts working on the business!

Although The Bell Tower on 34th experienced growth during its first few years in business—and we continue to experience growth—often we felt that Angela and I achieved success *despite* our partnership with Chuy. Our hard work, determination, and commitment were the constants that kept the company going.

It took a lot of thought and planning to figure out how to resolve our partner problem. Eventually, Angela and I offered to buy Chuy out, and he accepted. I strongly felt that we'd need to get him out of the picture before our business could reach its full potential for success.

Fortunately, after weeks of meetings and long emotional hours, not only did Chuy agree to a buy-out, he actually proposed a very agreeable method of payment: half of the money up front followed by monthly payments for the remaining amount, interest free.

Buying out Chuy was painful, and it was expensive, but at the end of the day, it had to be done—kind of like a root canal.

In 2015, after sending Chuy's final monthly payment, I called him and left him an angry message. I finally felt free to unleash my frustration. Frustration that he let Angela and me assume the lion's share of financial responsibility for the venue. Frustration over his less-than-helpful referrals. *Frustration that we'd paid him so much more than he ever contributed.*

Looking back, I realize I shouldn't have ended our business relationship that way. But I'd been wronged by a lot of people by then. And for the most part, few of them heard a word from me about it.

Chuy heard about it.

His response came as a text: "WOW."

He reminded me that he had been there when I really needed him. And he was right.

Back then, though, I felt strongly compelled to focus my energy on the business. I shifted my attention to the goal I'd set back in 2009, when Shrub and Branch agreed to my investment proposal. The plan had always been that Shrub and Branch would purchase the venue on West 34th Street, and I would complete its construction, open a business there, and be Shrub and Branch's tenant—for a few years. As soon as I was able, I would buy the venue from Shrub and Branch. Now, that final step was all that I could think about.

VICTORY!

About three years after we opened for business, The Bell Tower on 34th started to thrive even more. No longer were we renting chafing dishes and linens; we were able to buy our own. Not only that, we'd invested in state-of-the art appliances for our kitchen; we had phone lines; and we even had a pretty nice website.

Our staff had grown from one employee, Sarah, to an average of 80 to 100 employees, depending on the time of year.

Most importantly, we'd discovered ourselves, so to speak: We fine-tuned how we wanted to run the business. One of the most important things we did was to establish a company mission: delivering excellent events no one will ever forget. And everything we've done since then, from training and incentivizing staff to our approach to customer service, has been grounded in that objective.

We also have had the advantage of size—we can accommodate more than 350 guests per event—and the ability to provide customers with multiple rooms, whether they need them for different purposes (wedding ceremony, cocktail party, reception) or simply need extra space for large gatherings.

Our gorgeous building and grounds haven't hurt, either.

Before long, all of those factors came together. Sales increased steadily every year. When Angela and I parted ways with Chuy in 2012, my goal of buying the venue was just on the horizon. One year later, it was firmly in my grasp.

In August 2013, we bought The Bell Tower on 34th building and grounds from Shrub and Branch. That moment was our greatest confirmation yet that miracles are possible: We'd set an audacious goal, and with hard work, grit, the support of loved ones, and God's grace, *we achieved it!* Back in 2009, when I asked Shrub and Branch to consider my investment proposal, I suggested I knew how to make them $1 million dollars. All in all, including all of the rent payments we ever made to them and the purchase price, I estimate I had made them almost four times that amount.

Our growth has continued since that time. With the goal of purchasing the venue behind me, I've focused on finding new ways to strengthen the business and deliver excellent events. To do that, I've been enlisting the help of technology, a few special effects, and even some showbiz magic.

Bell Tower Trivia

IN 2013, THE YEAR WE BOUGHT THE BELL TOWER ON 34TH FROM OUR INVESTORS, OUR VENUE RECEIVED THREE MAJOR BRIDE'S CHOICE AWARDS AND WAS INDUCTED INTO THE HALL OF FAME BY WEDDING-PLANNING WEBSITE, THE KNOT. AT THIS WRITING WE HAVE RECEIVED MORE THAN 25 AWARDS, TOTAL, FOR OUR VENUE AND SERVICES INCLUDING 1ST PLACE OVERALL FOR THE NATIONAL ASSOCIATION FOR CATERING AND EVENTS (NACE).

Chapter 9

MAKING MAGIC

W HEN I TRADED BAND GIGS FOR REAL
estate transactions, I figured my days on stage
were essentially over.

Who would have guessed that I'd later build a career
behind the curtains? When you own an event venue,
one of the many hats you wear is stage manager: You're
constantly working behind the scenes to make every
moment sparkle.

For me, that role is one of the best parts of the job.
I've always loved the behind-the-scenes worlds of stage
and screen. There's something fascinating about the
unseen processes and technologies that create ambiance
and accentuate performances.

At The Bell Tower on 34th, we take our backstage
work very seriously. After all, if you're going to deliver

amazing events that no one will ever forget, you need to understand the value of showmanship. The same technologies that enhance a movie, musical, or film can also transform what could be merely nice moments at an event into something spectacular.

We've made it a priority to infuse a bit of show business magic into every event we've hosted since we opened. And after I transitioned from my building's tenant to its owner, I was able to devote considerably more resources to that effort. Little by little, we invested in state-of-the-art sound and lighting systems and, in some ways, transformed The Bell Tower on 34th into a movie set. Look up, and you'll see intricate lighting equipment suspended from an open grid ceiling. And while much of it is kept out of customers' sight, we use high-end audio systems at their events as well. As a result, our events have more sparkle and polish than ever.

I didn't want to stop with lights and sound, though. It was important for our staff to see that successful event production, in many ways, is another type of show business. Our people have roles to play in making sure everything customers experience at our venue is special. Memorable. Dazzling. So instead of sales people, we employ event producers. And instead of creating wedding floor plans, we work on set design. Most restaurants and event venues refer to their facilities in terms of "front of house" and "back of house." We have "on stage" and "back stage."

From what I see every day, these simple changes have contributed to our team members' drive to delight the customer, from personal interactions to the way they serve meals. They're focused on making every moment special.

With so many theatrical and cinematic elements in place, you could say the stage was set for the next chapter in our business' journey: an addition to The Bell Tower family. It was an opportunity to push forward toward even better, and more unforgettable, experiences for our customers.

BELL TOWER FILMS

It started with a chance meeting. I was catching up on paperwork the evening of a wedding when a young man walked into the office area where I was working. The man, Jason Adair, had been hired to make a video of the nuptials. He was looking for our house sound system.

Around that time, I was very interested in introducing a revolutionary new video service at The Bell Tower on 34th—I'll explain my idea in a moment—and I asked Jason about a device I'd read about that might help me do it.

Although he hadn't heard about that particular device, he was familiar with similar ones. As we chatted, I became increasingly impressed with Jason's knowledge of the events industry and video business. It was apparent that he also had a good sense of humor and was enthusiastic: qualities I value greatly. I could envision Jason becoming a friend and, eventually, a valuable part of our growing family at The Bell Tower on 34th.

About a year later, I knew how I wanted to work with

Jason and his skill set. I invited him to move into our old sales office—we'd since moved our sales and administrative staffs to a larger area on the property. I offered to provide Jason with free office space in exchange for occasional "help desk" tech support for our staff. By then, we were offering package deals with a wide range of potential add-ins, from use of our candelabras to event planning assistance, and I agreed to encourage our customers to add his photography and videography services to the event packages they purchased from us.

But I had even bigger plans for Jason. I wanted him to help me introduce the revolutionary idea I was mulling over when he and I first met. It called for bringing a brand-new level of videography services to the wedding industry: "live editing."

My thinking was, how awesome would it be if we could record events and edit the resulting video seamlessly, as events unfolded, and share the finalized videos with customers while they were still here?

Brides and grooms would be able to watch themselves exchanging vows as they ate dinner at their reception. And when they were ready to leave, the newlyweds and their guests would receive a thumb drive or link to a complete video of the day they'd just experienced, including the bride and groom's first dance, speeches, cutting of the cake—everything. We'd even post the video to customers' social media accounts if they wanted.

In those days this was unheard of. The competition wasn't doing that. No one was doing it.

The vehicle for this video magic would be a new

subsidiary: Bell Tower Films. It would start as the provider of our videography and photography services. And, eventually, I hoped, it would also offer my live-editing video product.

I invited Jason to head the new film company I formed and run it as its president. And, to my excitement, he accepted my offer without hesitation.

I have to say, it felt pretty cool to be able to tell people that The Bell Tower on 34th had its own film company. I got to introduce Jason to potential clients and explain that he was "President of Bell Tower Films, part of the Bell Tower family." It sounded pretty impressive.

For Jason, our arrangement was as good as it gets for a young entrepreneur. Although we weren't quite ready to market live editing, our sales people started selling his photography and videography services immediately. Jason also enjoyed free office space, along with use of my phone lines and Internet. I handled the legal end of establishing Bell Tower Films, and our accounting department took care of its billing.

Without question, we received a solid return on our investment. Jason stepped up when we needed basic tech support, and as a videographer and photographer, he provided quality products and services that added real value to what we, as a wedding venue, were doing for our customers.

As for my vision for live-editing video services, the leap into the unknown and unheard of...well, until recently, the product I had in mind was still unheard of.

Jason did come up with something we called

Real-Time Editing, but it was kind of pieced together. Basically, Jason simulated the effect I'd described. He'd record a wedding or event for a bit and then stop to send the footage to his editing room. There, his assistant worked on editing and putting segments together. Jason, meanwhile, would return to the event and continue recording. It was close, very close, but not quite the seamless flow of real time filming and editing I'd envisioned. On the bright side, we were able to impress our customers and their guests.

All in all, I think Jason and I had a very successful working relationship. It continued until late 2015, when Jason let us know he'd be moving to Dallas so his wife could accept a job there. After he left, Bell Tower Films went dormant for a while. In late 2016, we re-introduced one of the services our subsidiary had been providing: photo booths. Our sales team already had experience selling photo booths for Jason. It was a no-brainer.

To this day, photo booths are a popular feature with our customers. Still, I miss working with Jason, and I haven't given up on the hope of providing videos with live editing again someday.

MY NEPHEW WHO DOESN'T WORK FOR THE CIA

Jason wasn't the only young man to contribute to The Bell Tower on 34th's ability to dazzle customers. My nephew, Jared, laid a technological foundation for us that we continue to utilize today.

Jared, my sister Andrea's son, has always been interested in computers. Almost immediately after he earned his degree in computer engineering from Texas A&M University a few years ago, he was recruited for "government" work.

Apparently, he attended a family get together around that time, where Andrea proudly announced that Jared had gotten a job with the CIA. Jared quickly responded, "Mom, you're not supposed to tell anybody! It's supposed to be a secret!" I'm still not sure if he was joking or if he was serious.

Andrea, like any proud mom, didn't stop bragging on her son. She simply told people he worked for the Department of Defense.

I boasted about him, too, saying, "Don't tell anybody, but I think my nephew works for the CIA." When people asked me what he did for the CIA, I'd tell them that I wasn't quite sure, but it had to be important because Jared was a computer genius. That computer genius part wasn't an exaggeration, by the way. Jared really excels in that area, just like his dad, Kent. In fact, I still remember Kent mentioning, decades ago, that one day, we'd have the ability to carry our computer from room to room and remain connected to the Internet. What he was describing was Wi-Fi, a technology that I seem to recall he helped perpetuate.

Anyhow, Jared was happily not working for the CIA from San Antonio when a government shut-down occurred in October 2013. To this day, I'm not sure exactly how his work was affected, but it led Jared to give me a call. You should know that I'd been trying to lure Jared to The Bell Tower on 34th for quite some time. And now he had decided the time was right to take me up on my offer. At least for a while. According to him at the time, his long-term goal was to leave behind whatever technical work he was doing for the government, eventually relocate to China, and teach English. But that would require a work permit…and the ability to speak at least some Mandarin. I agreed to employ him while he worked on those things.

I already had a project for Jared in mind, the creation of another feature that would help set The Bell Tower on 34th apart from the competition.

The idea was that whenever someone called our business, they would receive a text from us, thanking them for contacting The Bell Tower on 34th, the instant they hung up. Those texts would help show potential customers the responsive, enthusiastic service they could expect from The Bell Tower on 34th. Jared set it up for us without a problem.

And he had some ideas of his own to put in place, too.

Jared's greatest priority was improving our email and Internet security, which made sense considering his background in government work. To get us to his high standards, he contributed to the early designs and helped build the beginnings of what would eventually become a hyper-speed, enterprise-level network capable of serving companies much larger than we were.

Not only was our network considerably more secure, Jared and business analyst Jose Cordova helped lay the groundwork for us to take customer service to an entirely new level. Consider our customer portal. Everyone who has a contract with us can log into the portal to manage guest lists and menus, review floor plans, make payments, make appointments with their event producer, and more.

And through that same portal, we've established an extensive collection of knowledge, an online encyclopedia of wedding and event advice—from etiquette dos and don'ts to planning guidelines—that customers can refer to around the clock.

All of those things supported our ability to keep on growing and improving The Bell Tower on 34th and to create unforgettable events that no one will forget. Along with many other contributors both inside and outside our company, Jared definitely helped to make those things possible.

After about a year with us, Jared achieved his goal of moving to China to become an English teacher. He later married a local woman there and is now a dad.

To this day, it's not clear to me if he still works for the U.S. government in some way. Or what exactly he did in San Antonio. All I know is Jared is a genius whiz kid phenom and a super great guy.

And I'll forever be grateful for the help of my nephew, Jared, who's not with the CIA.

Bell Tower Trivia

MULTIPLE SETS OF TWIN SISTERS HAVE
HELD THEIR WEDDINGS AT THE BELL
TOWER ON 34TH.

Chapter 10

OUR DAY IN COURT

WHILE MOST OF THE NEIGHBORHOOD surrounding The Bell Tower on 34th complements our business nicely, there has been one glaring exception: the cantina next door to our venue.

After several years of operating near the cantina, I became increasingly frustrated with its rough appearance and, even worse, the fights and shady-looking activity taking place in the parking lot late at night.

I started to wonder if any of the residents or other business owners in the neighborhood were troubled by the goings on there, too. After conducting a bit of online research in 2013, I found the answer was a resounding yes. A bunch of police calls had been made to the cantina over the years: calls about accidents, fights, and excessive noise well after 2 a.m., the standard closing time for bars.

I also learned that the cantina's state beer license was up for renewal. Normally, the state renews beer licenses automatically, but the Texas Alcoholic Beverage Commission (TABC) denies applications when there's evidence of illegal activity at the applicant's business. I already knew there had been illegal activity—the police records told the tale.

If I could just prove wrongdoings were still taking place at the cantina, I had a real chance of preventing a beer license renewal. And that, in turn, would force the owners to close or sell.

The result, hopefully, would be an end to the noise and unsavory activities in our neighborhood. I decided to take steps to make that happen.

First, I hired an attorney who specialized in TABC licensing and instructed him to file paperwork that protested the cantina's beer license renewal.

Before filing, the attorney did a bit of his own research and found old police reports about activities I hadn't even imagined were going on there: prostitution.

In my mind, our chances of preventing a beer license renewal had just skyrocketed. Now that I knew prostitution had taken place at the cantina in the past, I just needed proof that it was continuing. So, I hired a private investigator, a former Houston Police Department vice officer. He started going to the cantina at night and taking photos and video footage of activity in the parking lot, including multiple instances of money changing hands in what appeared to be drug and prostitution transactions.

Around the same time, some of my employees volunteered to circulate petitions around the neighborhood that called for the TABC to deny the cantina's beer license renewal. We easily got more than 100 signatures. That was enough, I hoped, to show that the cantina was a widespread concern in the neighborhood. People were fed up with the noise the cantina was generating, and they didn't like the idea of shady activity taking place so close to home.

We started turning to local leaders for additional help. The Texas Alcoholic Beverage Code gives county judges the authority to determine whether the state should grant a license to sell beer in their county. County judges also have the authority to approve or disapprove renewal applications. Our TABC lawyer arranged for us to meet with Laura Cahill, an assistant Harris County district attorney, so we could present her with our investigator's photos and video footage of potentially illegal transactions taking place in her county.

We also showed the photos and videos to our state representative, Jessica Farrar, and to Houston City Council Member Ellen Cohen, as well. I figured the more local leaders we had on our side, the more likely we were to stop the state from renewing the cantina's beer license. We would have shown our evidence to Texas Sen. John Whitmire, too, but he declined our invitations to meet.

In addition to the paperwork we filed with the TABC, we lodged a complaint with the county health department about the strong odors coming from the cantina's dumpster, and we contacted the fire marshal about the pallets and crates piled around the building. We also reported raw sewage in the parking lot, rodents on the property, smoking law violations our investigator witnessed (people were breaking city ordinances by smoking inside), and abandoned vehicles. And we provided photographic evidence for all of it.

Backing up our complaints was a detailed letter written by Larry Janda, the husband of Stephanie Janda, one of the grandchildren of former owner Bill Mraz. Larry, our property's former caretaker, wrote that he'd seen cantina customers trespassing and urinating on our grounds.

As we circulated our petition, we contacted local churches, the nearby YMCA, schools, and the neighborhood association to let them know what we were doing. And as the word began to spread, more people said they'd be willing to support our cause.

Eventually, we succeeded in getting a hearing, shortly before the Christmas holidays, in front of the Harris County Judge. It was our chance to make our case and attempt to convince the county judge to block the cantina's TABC license renewal.

Since there were so many of us, at least 100 people or more, I invited everyone to meet at The Bell Tower on 34th so we could arrive at the courthouse in force. I had "Cantina Go Away!" T-shirts made up for us, and we rode downtown to the courthouse in a bus I rented.

We had Bell Tower employees with us that day as well as neighbors, the assistant district attorney, and

Houston City Council representatives. We even had a former TABC regional director, who'd agreed to speak on our behalf. We filled the courtroom.

All-in-all, I'd spent between $10,000 and $20,000 to pull of this together, from the investigative work and attorney to our shirts.

Now we were going to have our day in court.

One by one, representatives from our group stood at the podium, made a short statement, and answered the judge's questions.

We showed video and had our investigator talk about what he saw taking place at the cantina parking lot.

Larry told the judge about the many people he'd seen trespassing and urinating on our property during the time he'd been a caretaker there many years before.

The hearing went on for several hours.

At the end of the day, we all went our separate ways. The judge said he'd make his decision known after the holidays.

At that point, I felt we'd made a strong case that illegal activity was taking place at the cantina, and I was fairly optimistic that the decision would be in our favor.

I was wrong.

A few weeks later, a local news channel reported that the judge ruled against blocking the cantina's beer license.

It sounded like the judge felt that because the cantina was in business before we opened The Bell Tower on 34th, we knew what we were getting ourselves into.

Now, we'd known ahead of our court date that the judge was very pro-business. We'd hoped that meant he'd be interested in protecting our business, and the others near us. Instead, it made him reluctant to do anything that would lead to a business closing.

I have to say, I was floored by how things went down.

Yes, a reasonable person has certain expectations when they locate near a bar or cantina. I might have expected some noise and occasional public drunkenness, but never illegal—and consistently disruptive—activities.

We had a state representative, people from the district attorney's office, and a former TABC leader, all saying there was no good reason the cantina should have its license renewed—with video to back it up—and the cantina owners still prevailed.

After the hearing, I realized I had to move on. Essentially, I'd been a one-man show, and I'd done everything I possibly could to put an end to the problems related to the cantina, at least at that point. Despite what felt like a setback, despite the noisy, law-evading neighbor, all I could do was concentrate on making The Bell Tower on 34th the best venue possible.

On the bright side, the cantina situation has improved. Immediately following the court hearing, the owners moved their front entrance so it no longer faces the street. They have cleaned up their parking lot, fixed up the outside of their building, and have a better system for cleaning their nearby dumpsters. Their music is much less of a nuisance, too.

It seems the hearing was a wake-up call to the cantina owners. They have decided to show more respect for the surrounding neighborhood. So, you could argue that our determination to push back against their bad behavior was a success.

Meanwhile, even though we weren't able to resolve the cantina situation exactly as we hoped, we remain dedicated to supporting our community. We do our best to be a good neighbor and responsible land owner.

Along with our large annual contributions to the area constable patrol programs, which neighborhoods pay for to bolster their security, we sponsor the annual Garden Oaks Wine Walk. The annual fundraiser helps Garden Oaks Civic Association cover the cost of their constable program.

We donate scholarship funds to Waltrip High School's athletic program, support the nearby Harriet and Joe Foster Family YMCA, and contribute monthly to Garden Oaks Baptist Church's general fund.

As a member of the North Shepherd Community Alliance, we help support responsible business development in our area. The alliance's efforts include an annual neighborhood garbage pick-up.

In addition, we regularly water and groom the beautiful greenery along the 34th street esplanade at our own expense.

We also support Trees for Houston's tree-planting efforts, and we are in the process of putting together a large donation to the group that will result in tree plantings and maintenance in our area.

Moreover, we've hosted events for the Center for Houston's Future, The Houston Symphony Conductors, The Houston Livestock Show and Rodeo and many more organizations, the kinds of events that help make Houston, Texas, proud.

Bell Tower Trivia

WE CAN'T MENTION ANY NAMES, BUT GUESTS AT OUR VENUE'S EVENTS OVER THE YEARS HAVE INCLUDED POLITICIANS, BILLIONAIRES, PROFESSIONAL ATHLETES AND WELL-KNOWN ACTORS, COMEDIANS, AND ENTERTAINERS.

Chapter 11

IN THE QUIET
MOMENTS

DAYLIGHT WAS MOMENTS AWAY WHEN
The Bell Tower employees Julio and Arnulfo had
an encounter with the inexplicable.

It was around 6:30 on a chilly morning in December
2016, and the men were getting a head start on setting
up our Chandelier Ballroom for an event. From their
position near the bar, both of them could see the
ballroom's entrance and the hallway leading to the
women's restroom.

So they had a perfect view when the bathroom door
popped open. On its own. Then, they say, the bathroom
lights came on and the fan started running. Almost
immediately, they heard the sound of the paper towel

machine dispensing folded hand towels, as if a customer had just finished washing up.

Except there were no customers in the building at the time. Or any other employees.

And that was the end of it. The men turned off the bathroom lights and fan, and no one—living or otherwise—attempted to turn them back on.

As incredible as that experience was, Arnulfo and Julio can take comfort in the fact that their colleagues won't be poking fun at them for sharing that story, or even questioning what they described.

Dozens of our employees have similar stories of their own, and many of them occurred in or near our Chandelier Ballroom, known by staff as "the Chandelier."

At one point, I asked staff members who've observed paranormal activity to let me videotape them as they shared their stories. About half a dozen people agreed to participate. Some of them asked me not to reveal their names.

One employee who shared her story, Katie, described a moment that could have been ripped from the *Ghost Hunters* TV show. She and Sarah (my first Bell Tower employee) were about to review security camera footage of a recent event when they noticed that our motion-activated cameras had captured a large block of activity at 3 a.m., long after the event ended and our staff had left for the night. They took a look.

"All of a sudden I see this little sphere thing," Katie says. "At first, I thought it was just a little spot on the camera, but it started moving…It floated over to the pavilion doors that were locked from the outside, and you can literally see the doors getting pushed. And then, it went into the Chandelier, so we started switching cameras to try to find it. It just floated through the building. The entire time we're thinking, 'This shouldn't be setting off cameras.' But it did."

Another interviewee, Jose, has his own tale of encountering a spectral female. It was his second day on double shifts and he was wiped out. Between events, he had decided to grab a nap in the chapel. When he woke, he saw a woman in a dress walking *above* the ground, from the balconies to the opposite end of the room. It was a sight, he says, he'll never forget.

Other employees described moments when they were working alone and heard approaching footsteps. In each instance, they looked, and no one was there. One employee had the inescapable sense he was being followed. And another saw a man leap behind our supply shed door. He never emerged, and when she looked behind the door, no one was there.

Even construction workers who were on the grounds before we opened had reported sightings of ghosts walking the property at dusk.

BACK IN THE DAY

The fact is, our property's supernatural stories date back long before the days of The Bell Tower. In fact, Larry Janda shared a couple with me. As I've mentioned, Larry's ex-wife, Stephanie Janda, is the granddaughter of the late Bill Mraz, whose dance hall sat on this site from the 1940s until it burned down in 2004. The Mraz Dance Hall was a historical landmark and major social gathering place for Czech-Americans. During its last few years in business, Stephanie and Larry owned and operated it.

During that period, Larry says, he frequently worked at the dance hall alone and never felt uncomfortable. But he did have an experience he can't explain.

"I felt reasonably certain that I heard someone whistling in the hall while I was working there," he says. "I was working in the bathrooms, cleaning up, alone. I thought I heard someone whistling, and when I went out to investigate no one was there.

"It was a happy whistle, kind of a 'Whistle While You Work' kind of tune. It was kind of faint, because I was in the bathroom, but it was enough that it made me come out and look."

Stephanie told Larry of her own mysterious experience on the property. While some people may find supernatural encounters unnerving, Stephanie didn't find hers creepy or strange at all. Instead, she said, it was heart-warming. Stephanie, who adored her grandfather, has distinct childhood memories of the aroma that emanated from Bill's accordion case when he opened it. "It resonated with her, and she never forgot it," Larry says. "She claims that one day when she was in the hall she smelled that smell. It was very vivid to her, so she felt like her grandfather was there. Again, that was a happy thing."

BRINGING IN REINFORCEMENTS

Unfortunately, my staff members were less than positive about their encounters. After repeated reports of para-normal encounters by my employees, I arranged for Lura Lovestar to visit the property. Lura had experience "cleansing" sites of spiritual activity.

Lura Lovestar

I'm not sure if I believe in ghosts, but I had no reason to doubt what my employees told me over the years. They clearly believed what they told me and had no reason to lie. I wanted them to feel safe and happy when they're here. And I certainly didn't want customers to worry about ghostly party crashers during one of the most important days of their lives. If there was a chance I could do something to help, I had to take it. That's why I decided to seek Lura Lovestar's help. Chuy, still a partner at the time, said he'd had good results with her as an energy expert. After he heard about the experiences some of our workers were having, he practically demanded that we bring Lura in.

After Lura toured the property, she and I discussed the location of our venue. Not far from us is a funeral home, as well as a Catholic church where funeral services are held. If spirits have lingered in this area, maybe The Bell Tower struck them as a pleasant resting spot. Another possibility is that something dramatic took place in this area years ago, and it triggered paranormal activity. Or, more likely, the things our employees have described and the reasons behind them are simply beyond our knowledge or understanding.

I can't really explain what Lura did, beyond praying and applying essential oil here and there, but her visit did seem to help. Reports of supernatural activity subsided after she walked through our property. Lura encouraged me to bring her back from time to time for additional "touch ups," which we have done, and I think we'll do it again. It certainly doesn't hurt.

Bell Tower Trivia

DURING CONSTRUCTION, IT RAINED EVERY TIME WE WERE ALMOST READY TO POUR THE BUILDING'S FOUNDATION. IT RAINED 24 OUT OF 30 DAYS. WE WERE REPEATEDLY FORCED TO START OVER AGAIN, REMOVING THE FOUNDATION'S STEEL FRAME, CLEANING OUT THE MUD, AND PUTTING THE STEEL IN PLACE AGAIN. EVENTUALLY WE DECIDED ON A 24-HOUR SCHEDULE. ONE MORNING, I ARRIVED AT THE JOB SITE TO FIND ONLY A FEW WORKERS THERE AND VERY LITTLE PROGRESS ON THE FOUNDATION. WHEN I ASKED WHY, THE ANSWER I GOT WAS THAT TWO GHOSTS HAD BEEN SEEN WALKING THE PROPERTY, AND IT SCARED THE WORKERS OFF. AT THAT TIME, WE HAD NO IDEA THE PROPERTY HAD A REPUTATION FOR PARANOR-MAL ACTIVITY. MAYBE THE WORKERS SAW THE GHOSTS OF MR. AND MRS. MRAZ WALKING THE PROPERTY AND GUARDING THEIR BURIED TREASURE!

Chapter 12

A GUIDED TOUR

"Wow!!! The venue was absolutely beautiful...the food was incredible...everyone raved about the place...extremely helpful...made it so easy!!"

THE SENTIMENT OF THAT BRIDE HAS BEEN echoed by many of our visitors, from wedding guests to business execs. When I hear comments like hers, I know that all of the ups and downs, missteps, and false starts we endured are long behind us. And while we haven't achieved perfection—I'm always working toward that—we have realized the goal I set when we opened The Bell Tower on 34th. We kept on going; we refused to give up. And now we're delivering excellent events that no one will ever forget.

How do we do it? How do we delight our clients and their guests every day? Well, for starters, we incorporate time-tested processes into nearly everything we do; we cultivate highly motivated, well-trained staff who've been equipped with all of the tools they need to give visitors their best; and in many cases, we tap into the power of state-of-the-art technology.

Let me take you on a guided tour of The Bell Tower and show you!

WHERE THE MAGIC HAPPENS

"The entire wedding was absolutely dreamy, breathtaking, and more than I could have ever hoped for! It was the most magical weekend!! I feel lucky to say I had my dream wedding at The Bell Tower!"

Remember the Cantera stone that Evil Dan and I searched for in Mexico? As you walk through our ballrooms and chapels, you'll see many features made from this beautiful element. The stone, which we've incorporated into our walls, frames, and other elements of the building, contributes to an Old World feel and beauty that surrounds guests throughout their time with us.

The ballroom areas also feature sections of walls and ceilings crafted from "Old Chicago Brick," reclaimed from late 19th century Chicago, after a massive fire devastated the city. The brick's terra cotta tones, from light pink to salmon, add warmth, texture, and color to our events' atmosphere.

The flooring throughout most of the building is an expensive type of marble imported from Turkey:

Enhancing the beauty of this room is the lovely French chandelier that Angela's mom, Glenda Nicholson, helped us acquire. The room also features spacious arched windows and bricked arch ceilings. ©Stephanie Rogers

Turkish Travertine. It complements the other natural elements in the room and further enhances the look and feel of events—as they unfold and in photos and videos.

One of the most stunning features you'll see is our huge iron chandelier, possibly the largest of its kind in Texas, displayed in the appropriately named "Chandelier Ballroom."

The chandelier is another treasure from the Mexico trip I made with Evil Dan. Hundreds of couples have shared their first dance under this striking, hand-crafted light fixture. Its presence adds a touch of romance to every reception, celebration, and event held in its midst.

We have tried to weave elements of the stage and screen into our events: We understand the importance of "set design." That's why you'll find special elements like the chandelier in all of our event rooms. It's the reason for the impressive 16-foot-tall doors in the Candela ballroom, which were made of mahogany by our onsite maintenance team.

Each element adds a touch of drama and style to our customers' special day—from our sweeping stone staircases to our building's high ceilings, Italian archways, wood-burning fireplaces, and balconies. Customers repeatedly tell me that our rooms are so stunning that they barely needed to decorate them for their events here.

The chapel areas, where wedding ceremonies, smaller receptions, and other special events are held, feature similar architectural features but provide a more intimate, reverent feel. These rooms lend themselves to ceremonies of all kinds, for customers of all faiths and beliefs.

We've applied equal attention to the areas where brides prepare for the magic ahead of them. Our elegant dressing rooms were designed by Angela's mom, Glenda Nicholson, with comfort in mind. Every luxurious element conveys a message to the bride: "You are special, and this is your day to shine."

We understand the importance of combining beauty with function. That's why we use technology to manage the house. We're constantly working to prevent unwanted surprises and to enhance guests' comfort and enjoyment.

You'll see that our dance floors, for example, feature contemporary, strategically placed lighting that energizes celebrations. Brides love the fact they can colorize the floor for added fun.

Our stunning floors provide one of many beautiful backdrops for your event photos. ©Joey T Photography

Our Chandelier Ballroom. ©Blanca Duran

Our staircases are perfect for making grand entrances.
©Jessica Pledger

We have seven different dressing rooms. This is our spacious
"Fancy Dressing Room."

And the ballrooms are equipped with mounted touch-screen tablets that we can use to manage music, other sound elements, lighting and room temperatures, so our visitors can focus on having fun.

We make it a priority to appeal to all of our guests' senses while they're here. So, in addition to the venue's lovely surroundings, we provide pleasant sounds as well. That runs the gamut from the music soundtrack we play (when it doesn't interfere with events) to the strong, clear sound quality we provide everywhere that guests are.

WALK AROUND THE GROUNDS

Step outside and into our lush gardens where brides can steal away for a few tranquil moments before their ceremony begins. Many couples make this setting the backdrop for enchanted, fairy-tale weddings.

We've found that the sound of our 30-foot tall cascading water wall, one of our couples' favorite backdrops for photos and outdoor ceremonies, helps create a relaxing, meditative environment for guests.

I hand-picked and oversaw the planting of every oak tree on our property, including a giant oak in the Candela courtyard: It had to be lifted over the fountain walls by crane before it could be installed.

As you stroll the grounds, you may notice the Rolls-Royce parked to the side of the building. This is one of the cars we offer as an add-on transportation service. In today's Uber and Lyft world, offering the valet service is yet another way we differentiate The Bell Tower on

Our grounds are designed to create a relaxing, meditative environment. ©Agape Photography

34th from other venues. When wedding guests and event-goers need us to give them a ride from their hotels to our venue, they arrive in style, in this classic, 1960 Rolls-Royce vehicle.

Whether people are here for a wedding or a business meeting, stress levels can be high. That's why we strive to offer a soothing, natural environment for those who come here.

Because we're dedicated to keeping our property picture-perfect for guests, we employ specialized staff who are dedicated to providing constant maintenance, inside and out. Some of these employees have been with us for 15 years or more. We have a close working relationship, and they share our goal of delivering unforgettable events.

We can illuminate our water wall in white or colored light.
©Nate Messarra

We planted every tree here after purchasing the property,
including Italian cypress trees, oaks, bamboos, and palms.
©Real Teel Photography

REMINDERS OF ANOTHER ERA

Our grounds also reveal glimpses of our property's history. A short walk away from the main building are two houses left over from the days when this was the site of the Bill Mraz Dance Hall. Bill's family lived on the ground for years. Along with the houses, we've kept what remained of the dance hall: a brick garage that didn't burn down when fire devastated the property in December 2004.

Nearby is the place where a giant elm tree used to tower above Bill's barbecue pit—he loved preparing meat and barbecuing for friends, family, and guests.

Not far from the houses on our grounds is a large maintenance shed where we store a vast array of items guests can rent for their events, from extra chairs and tables to outdoor propane heaters. In some ways, you could say we're a one-stop shop for customers planning an event. They will find we can provide nearly any and every element they could possibly need, making their preparations considerably more convenient.

BEHIND-THE-SCENES

"Even better than the sheer beauty of the venue was the customer service...we received outstanding service...I could not have been happier with the outcome of the most important day of my life."

As I've mentioned, in some ways, our business has evolved from a wedding and event venue into a tech company that hosts weddings and special events. The technology isn't always obvious to our customers, but it's woven into nearly every facet of what we do here. In many cases, it's what allows us to deliver unforgettable experiences.

Take our employee work areas. We've mounted several large flat screens that display a social media feed specifically for our business. This cascading stream of information helps our team members stay on top of each event and the last-minute curveballs that can come with them, so we can keep everyone's special day running smoothly.

We also use fancy software to manage employee scheduling. Our system is designed to ensure that each event is fully staffed, and at the same time, to accommodate our staff members' needs.

BELL TOWER BENEFITS

MY PHILOSOPHY HAS ALWAYS BEEN THAT taking good care of my staff results in better events. I do that by offering unique benefits (free flu shots, CPR training, flexible scheduling, money for good grades on report cards, spending money toward employee outings), hosting special events just for staff, and by maintaining open communications.

Because we strive to take a hands-on approach to leadership, mentoring, and team-building, we have also scheduled events like "Pizza With Roger" for example, where employees and I talk about their needs, their goals, and how I can support them.

We offer traditional benefits, too, including health insurance and a 401k program with increasing company matches.

PROCESSES IN PLACE

"Everything flowed smoothly, and I did not worry about a single thing...guests are still raving about how much they enjoyed themselves...such a wonderful, magical experience."

When customers tell us that their event went flawlessly, we know why: We've designed a multitude of processes that help ensure the best customer experience possible. You'll see evidence of them throughout our employee areas.

Our Year to Date (YTD) information chart, for example, tracks the resources we sell customers during the course of the year, including liquor, food, and linens as part of their event packages. Not only are we focused on strong sales, we're dedicated to being good stewards of the supplies people purchase from us. So we continue passing food and drinks throughout events to make sure nothing is wasted. We monitor food and liquor supplies, too, and alert managers and the chef if they're running low on something. We're dedicated to keeping guests comfortable, well-fed, and happy while they're here.

> *"Everything was very professional…I was able to just relax and enjoy the day. The food was very good and many of the guests complimented not only the menu but the service and the entire venue. It would have been hard to find a more elegant place to be married."*

Our processes also ensure the best service possible. That's the purpose of the event manager report cards that employees see near the YTD display backstage. Event managers are senior servers who are charged with supervising, motivating, and training the other servers on their team. The report cards consider factors like promptness, neatness, accuracy, and professionalism, among other items. And because one of my duties is motivating the event managers, I try to take them all out for dinner once a year at Carrabba's, where I tell them about the time I asked restaurant co-founder and chef Johnny Carrabba to pretend he knew me. That story is a great illustration of the value of keeping your wits and taking chances, even when it seems the odds are against you.

One especially effective internal process is the highly detailed checklist system we use for every event we deliver. The list, another item that you'll see displayed in the employee work areas, includes customized "to-dos" for every step that plays a role in presenting an event. It encompasses every aspect of the tasks we perform, from prep work to our interactions with our customers and their guests. I can't share too many details; we might even take steps to patent this system. What I can tell you is, by checking off every box on our list, we know we're delivering excellent events without fail.

One of the things I've learned during my years in business is that empowering employees with the right training and tools—and the freedom to make things right, on the spot—results in the best possible results for customers. So, yes, our team members are given checklists and specific tasks, but how they achieve them is up to them. Employees know that they're free to make "executive decisions" on the job as long as they support our objective: to deliver an excellent event.

KITCHEN

"Three weeks after the wedding, and people are still raving about the food!"

The "star attraction" of our kitchen is our Rational

Smart Oven with a SelfCookingCenter®. This oven can be pre-set for any item on our menu. It knows how long to cook, at what temperature, and how much moisture or smoke to pipe in. It's considered one of the world's top three smart ovens. And it guarantees that every meal is cooked to perfection, even when we're serving a dinner for hundreds.

HOW FAR WE'VE COME

IN SOME WAYS, OUR KITCHEN IS A VISUAL testament to the progress we've made since we first opened The Bell Tower on 34th.

During our first year in business, we didn't have much of a kitchen. We relied on an apartment-style, four-burner electric stove with a single oven under it to prepare meals. That's one of the reasons I'm so proud of the state-of-the-art Rational Smart Oven. In the early days we even had to boil water and serve instant coffee because we didn't have a coffee maker.

Because our budget was so tight in the beginning, we rented our silverware. And after we could afford to buy our own, we polished it by hand. Now, we have an automated polisher that ensures guests have dazzling silverware at every table.

The same can be said of our approach to dishes. We went from renting them, to washing the dishes we purchased in a three-compartment sink, to eventually using a state-of-the art Ecolab dishwasher for consistently sparkling place settings. The Ecolab is capable of washing 1,000 place settings worth of dishes every four hours, which allows staff to quickly close or reset the inventory at the end of each shift.

The two massive walk-in coolers in our kitchen tell a story, too. We started with one, but as we grew, we quickly outgrew it. For a while, we had to rent 18-wheelers with coolers to store our food. These days, our twin coolers have the capacity to hold a large volume of fresh groceries, a must for us to be able to serve over 50,000 guests annually.

The kitchen also is where employees clock in and out. When we opened the venue, we had a manual time clock. Now we have biometric timing equipment that identifies employees by fingerprint as they begin and end their shifts. The technology ties in with the payroll software we use. This is technology that was considered leading edge when we first adopted it. Not anymore!

Every time we invest in bigger and better kitchen equipment, it frees up more of our staff members' time, time that they can spend on making sure our guests are having an amazing event.

Of course, technology only carries you so far when it comes to preparing cuisine. This is one of those areas that relies on human skill and creativity. We are very fortunate at The Bell Tower on 34th. Not only have we moved beyond the days when investing in kitchen equipment was beyond our reach, we've also progressed past the chef uncertainties we experienced in our early days. We don't have to worry anymore about wooing a celebrity chef to please potential investors or scrambling to buy take-out chicken marinara to cover for a temperamental chef. I'm consistently impressed with our executive chef's cooking, and more importantly, so are our customers.

PREVENTIVE MEASURES

Another thing you might notice as we stroll through the kitchen is a collection of clickers, which our servers use to take periodic headcounts during an event. If we find that a customer has more guests than they expected, we can take steps to make sure the customer's event still has enough food, chairs, tables, linens, and other supplies. Our policy for overages is included in our customer agreement.

We've learned that no matter how well planned an event is, odds are that something unexpected will happen. We have processes and supplies in place to address as many of those unwelcome surprises as possible.

For one thing, we maintain an "event cabinet" not far from the kitchen. The cabinet is stocked with the items customers most commonly forget, including bobby pins, tampons, buttons, bra strap clips, reading glasses, toothbrushes, hairbrushes, and more.

We also have multiple ice machines and an emergency ice supplier on call whenever we host an event.

LAUNDRY ROOM

Another area with state-of-the-art technology is our laundry room, which has the latest washer and dryer technology for maximum efficiency, along with motion-sensor-controlled lighting, which helps us manage costs.

The majority of items washed here are linens. In most cases, event tables are covered with two pieces of linen: a large white tablecloth and a smaller overlay. We launder the tablecloths and rent the overlays.

We maintain status reports on linen usage to prevent waste: We try to only use and wash exactly what's needed. Before long it will be time for yet another upgrade in this area of the business.

OFFICE AREAS

"Someone has put a lot of thought into making this the perfect wedding venue."

Our upstairs offices function as the mission control center for many of our technological features. The original computer servers developed by my nephew Jared (who doesn't work for the CIA) were housed here. After Jared moved to China, we built upon the technological foundation that he helped establish for us. A few years ago, we created The Bell Tower Customer Hub, where people can manage nearly every aspect of their event, including scheduled tastings, onsite portraits, floor plans, menu selections, payments, and vendors. Customers can use the hub to schedule appointments with their event producers, too.

We also developed a cloud-based knowledge repository that brides can access through the FAQ widget on The Bell Tower Customer Hub. The knowledge base is more than an FAQ page, though. Our event producers worked together to compile an exhaustive list of the questions they've received over the years, along with their answers, so customers can benefit from their insights and experience. Users type in questions, much

It's a joy to exhibit Angela's beautiful paintings (above and below) in our venue.

like they would begin a search on Google. In most cases, an answer pops up before they've finished typing. If, for any reason, the knowledge base doesn't have an answer to a question, our event producers can step in and find the information the client needs.

Another online feature we provide is our event countdown clock, accessible through the Customer Hub. The clock helps people schedule and manage their to-dos as they approach their big day.

So, while we're utilizing technology to create unforgettable events, we're also helping our customers harness technology to make their planning process easier and more effective.

ADMINISTRATIVE OFFICES

In addition to our upstairs offices, we have a second set of offices in another part of our building, which was left over from the Bill Mraz Dance Hall days. Our budget was so tight during our early days in business that I wasn't even sure I could afford to buy a file cabinet. In the end, I decided to bet on our success: I bought two of them. These days, everyone in the office staff has their own filing cabinets, along with a large one that's shared. File cabinets might sound a bit antiquated for a tech company that hosts events, but they tie in with the "be prepared" approach I described earlier. Because we haven't discarded "old school" record keeping, we still have access to important documents, agreements, and schedules if a hurricane hits or the power goes out.

MY OFFICE

My office walls are lined with photos and mementos that hold special meaning. They include a photo that our gardener, Pedro, provided of his family's house in Guatemala.

Why is this photo an important part of my office décor? The story is simple: Pedro is one of our crew who is responsible for the lush beauty of our trees and flowers, and he sends a portion of his weekly earnings back to his family in Guatemala. They've used the funds to build a beautiful and very large home. The picture of his house (still in progress) is a reminder to me of our company's impact for good on team members' lives. It also is a source of inspiration: I like to reference the photo to staff and encourage them to dream big and never give up because anything is possible.

Also on the wall is an aerial photo of our building, while it was still under construction, taken from a drone. This shot reminds me how far we've advanced, and how many obstacles we've overcome, since I started building this venue.

Then there's my celebration of all things "34." My collection includes a No. 34 Houston Oilers jersey autographed by the legendary Earl Campbell, the hugely talented running back fondly referred to as "The Human Wrecking Ball" during his pro-football days. (The Houston Oilers, for those of you too young to remember, was Houston's pro football team from 1960 to 1996, when they moved and became the Tennessee Titans.)

Our gardener, Pedro, has been building this beautiful house in Guatemala with his money he's saved from his earnings.

You could say I was on the top of the world when our venue was under construction.

I recently took it home, but I also have a photo of my son, a Little League pitcher, in his No. 34 jersey. The team members had the option of choosing their numbers. In my son's case, the decision was a no-brainer.

I don't actively search for 34-themed memorabilia, but when I come across a good addition to my collection, I rarely can resist grabbing it up.

Not only am I grateful for our past—and the results of our commitment to keep on going—I'm also excited about my vision for The Bell Tower on 34th's future.

*An "all things 34" collector's dream photo: Walter Payton of the
Chicago Bears and Earl Campbell of the Houston Oilers. I also
have an Earl Campbell jersey (below).*

More from my "all things 34" collection: Above is my Hakeem "The Dream" Olajuwon jersey. Hakeem, who played for the Houston Rockets, was the NBA's Defensive Player of the Year for the 1992–93 and 1993–94 seasons and was also the league's Most Valuable Player (MVP) in 1993–94. I'm equally proud of my Nolan Ryan jersey (below). I love the fact that the Houston Astros retired Nolan's number. The Hall of Fame pitcher was with the 'Stros 1980-88.

Bell Tower Trivia

ONE OF THE MOST COMMONLY REQUESTED ITEMS FROM OUR "EVENT CABINET" IS A SAFETY PIN.

CLOSING THOUGHTS

I've been careful while writing the history of The Bell Tower on 34th to avoid suggesting that we've achieved all of our objectives.

Don't get me wrong, I'm tremendously grateful for The Bell Tower and the fact that with encouragement, God's grace, and lots of determination, we've been able to overcome a seemingly unending stream of challenges to get to this point.

But at the time of writing this, I don't consider our journey complete. Not even close.

There is still so much I see we need to do as a company. In the beginning I wanted to make the building into *what it was always meant to be*—a fantastic location for weddings and special events. But we have been working toward something even more special. And that is the vision I have for the direction of the company. I still have very big ideas and goals for our operation in my sights, and they're very doable because we have such a strong business model, a fantastic prototype, and a great team. Our back-end processes—from the way we train employees to the detailed checklists we have in place to make sure every event is unforgettable—make our business very scalable. I'm confident that, when the timing is right, the processes that make events come together so seamlessly at our current location can be just as effective at other locations *all over the world.*

The key to having more locations around the world is establishing a strong second location. The next location will serve as a proof of concept: It will show that the policies and procedures that we developed really work, even in other geographical areas with different people. But I won't even consider opening a second location until I'm convinced we're ready. I work on getting us ready every day—all of us at The Bell Tower do. We're continuously improving upon our processes and manuals and training systems in every area of our business, whether it's the food and beverage side, finance, or sales and marketing. And when we're ready, we'll be able to reproduce our prototype and our company culture to create even more thriving locations. I know we'll need some tweaks here and there when we open our next location, but that's OK. As soon as our next location is on solid ground, I expect the process of opening locations No. 3, 4, and 5 will be relatively smoother.

By the time we have location No. 5 in place, there's a good chance I'll be nearing retirement age. We will make sure that the deal structures for the next generation of locations will allow me to share my responsibilities with other trusted individuals.

ROGER, THE CEO

I said earlier that it doesn't feel right to suggest I've reached a point where I feel our company is good enough, or that we've achieved any kind of "happily-ever-after." Part of that stems from my mindset as CEO: I'm never satisfied. I'm not saying I'm ungrateful or perpetually unhappy. It's just that *I never feel we're quite good enough.* I never feel we're in a spot where we can take a breath and relax. I've tried to sit back and enjoy how far we've come and enjoy how beautiful the building and grounds are, how happy the people here are, and how smoothly the operation runs. I just can't do it. It's not who I am. I'm always looking for a better way to do things. *What if we laid out our gardens this way? What if we used that technology for climate control?* I'm continuously in the mode of fine tuning. This could be a character flaw or something people associate with an undiagnosed obsessive-compulsive issue. But that doesn't matter. I'm on a mission to make this business the best it can be for the leader who comes after me, and I only have so much time to do that.

I don't want my successor—whether it's my wife, one of my kids, or an employee who steps up—to say, "Why didn't Dad do this?" or "Why didn't Roger take care of that?" I don't want anything undecided or undone. Of course, there will be some decisions the next person will have to make, some loose ends. But I don't want there to be a major hole or gap in what I leave behind. I want people to say, "Wow, Roger left us a very well-oiled machine, a very well-run company with very little left undone."

Not only am I focused on the business I pass on to my successor, I expect the people who work here to develop a similar mindset. If everyone in this place looks for ways to fine tune the processes that they pass on to their successors, it makes our business stronger and helps the people who work here grow professionally. I'm open to the idea of someone who starts in an entry-level position like dishwasher or busser—someone with a strong work ethic, vision, and grit—to move up through the ranks and eventually become the leader of the company. I think anyone we hire should eventually be able to run this place.

Anyway, while I tend to spend a lot of time evaluating how The Bell Tower is doing now and planning for the future, writing this book has forced me to spend some time looking back, too. And that's worthwhile. It's important to remember where you came from and how you got here. As a CEO, you've got to have vision, purpose, and values. You have to have a plan for what you're going to accomplish, and being mindful of where you started is part of that.

I hope whoever follows me as The Bell Tower CEO uses this book to better understand how we got to this point: why we do the things we do. Maybe they'll write an amendment for their successor.

As for me, my journey during the last 10-plus years certainly has been intense. I don't think that I've changed as a person, but I have, perhaps, become more sensitive to the needs of the people who count on me. I've always wanted to take good care of my employees, suppliers, and vendors, but that has become even more important to me after experiencing the devastating repercussions of working for thoughtless employers and clients, as I have.

I've also seen, firsthand, what it means when someone steps into your life and gives you a chance to make things better for yourself and your family. That's what Shrub and Branch did for me when they originally invested in me so many years ago. So these days, I'm acutely aware of the great responsibility I have and the far-reaching effects my actions can have on others. I want to use the blessings and influence I've received to do good things for our stakeholders, including our employees and their family members, the vendors who provide goods and services to our business, and the customers who entrust us with their important events on a day-to-day basis.

It's a big task to live up to all of those responsibilities, *and it's super humbling to know there are so many people counting on you and your decisions* when you're in my position.

Because I'm determined to make careful and informed decisions, I believe it's my duty and responsibility to surround myself with smarter people who can accomplish more than I can, who can join us in our vision for The Bell Tower and help us realize our short-, medium-, and long-term goals—even in the face of challenges.

THE FUEL BEHIND THE GROWTH

I should point out that my vision for The Bell Tower is about more than what I want to accomplish—it's also about what I want to prevent. I have a deep-seated desire to make sure what happened at this place under its previous management never happens again. I'll do whatever it takes to make sure there's never another catastrophe like The Brides of Harris County—or the kind of personal tragedy my family and I experienced when we sunk into bankruptcy—on my watch. That's been a powerful driver to make this business rock-solid and long-lasting. We've been making lemons into lemonade in a big way.

I also want to emphasize the role of God, and of those closest to me, in this unfolding story.

What we have now is the direct result of Angela, who gave me her blessings to go forward with this business endeavor; the unwavering support of friends and family; the prayers of my mother, and—above all—grace and blessings from God. That's nothing to be taken lightly. At the end of the day, I believe everything my family and I went through was for a reason. And now God has put me in a position where I can, hopefully, do meaningful good for others.

BIBLIOGRAPHY

Aldon S. Lang and Christopher Long, *Handbook of Texas Online*, "LAND GRANTS," accessed June 9, 2017, http://www.tsha-online.org/handbook/online/articles/mpl01.

Archive.today webpage capture, "Bill Mraz Dance Hall," accessed June 22, 2017, https://archive.li/5ZRJ1.

Barker, Eugene C., *Handbook of Texas Online*, "AUSTIN, STEPHEN FULLER," accessed June 9, 2017, https://tshaon-line.org/handbook/online/articles/fau14.

Culbertson, Margaret, *Offcite*, "Some Assembly Required," accessed Sept. 9, 2018, http://offcite.org/wp-content/uploads/sites/3/2010/03/SomeAssemblyRequired_Culbertson_Cite54.pdf.

Glenn, Mike, *Houston Chronicle*, "A Houston tradition dies in Polka Hall Fire," accessed June 22, 2017, https://www.chron.com/news/houston-texas/article/A-Houston-tradition-dies-in-polka-hall-fire-1962825.php.

Gracy II, David B., *Handbook of Texas Online*, "AUSTIN, MOSES," accessed June 9, 2017, https://tshaonline.org/handbook/online/articles/fau12.

Handbook of Texas Online, "MORTON, WILLIAM," accessed June 21, 2017, http://www.tshaonline.org/handbook/online/articles/fmo70.

Hinton, Marks, *Historic Houston Streets: The Stories Behind the Names*, Bright Sky Press, Houston, Texas, 2012.

Hlavaty, Craig, *Houston Chronicle*, "Hurricane Ike hit the Houston and Galveston areas a decade ago this week," accessed February 25, 2019, https://www.chron.com/news/houston-texas/houston/amp/Hurricane-Ike-hit-the-Houston-and-Galveston-areas-9219780.php.

Life on the Brazos River, "Morton Family," accessed June 21, 2017, http://lifeonthebrazosriver.com/TheMortonFamily.htm.

Life on the Brazos River, "Nancy Morton," accessed June 21, 2017, http://lifeonthebrazosriver.com/NancyMorton.htm.

Noonoo, Jemimah, *Houston Chronicle*, "Couples Get Weddings of Their Dreams," accessed May 21, 2017, https://www.chron.com/life/article/Couples-get-weddings-of-their-dreams-1633114.php.

PBS, "THE WEST, Episode 2 (1806-1848): Empire Upon the Trails," accessed June 9, 2017, https://www.pbs.org/weta/thewest/program/episodes/two/tejas.htm.

PBS, "New Perspectives on THE WEST: Stephen Austin Fuller," accessed June 9, 2017, https://www.pbs.org/weta/thewest/people/a_c/austin.htm.

Shady Acres Houston, Texas, History, accessed June 22, 2017, https://www.shadyacres.org/history.

Sowell, Andrew Jackson, *History of Fort Bend County*, Coyle & Co., 1904.

State Historical Society of Missouri, "Historic Missourians: Moses Austin," accessed June 9, 2017, https://shsmo.org/historicmissourians/name/a/austin.

Stewart Title Company, Abstract of Title Search: 2013.

Texas Archival Resources Online, "A Guide to The Austin's Colony Records, 1823-1841," accessed June 9, 2017, https://legacy.lib.utexas.edu/taro/txglo/00053/glo-00053.html.

Texas General Land Office, "History of Texas Public Lands," accessed June 9, 2017, http://www.glo.texas.gov/history/archives/forms/files/history-of-texas-public-lands.pdf.

Texas General Land Office, Land Grant Search: 2017.

The Heritage Society, *Absolutely Memorial*, "A Little Piece of History: The Heart of a Community," accessed Feb. 25, 2019, https://issuu.com/absolutelymemorial/docs/memorial-may-2017.

The Heritage Society at Sam Houston Park, St. John Church, accessed July 2, 2017, https://www.heritagesociety.org/stjohn-church.

Worrall, Dan, *Pleasant Bend: Upper Buffalo Bayou and the San Felipe Trail in the Nineteenth Century,* Concertina Press, Fulshear, Texas, 2016.